MW01489024

"We Shocked the World!"

A Case Study of Jesse Ventura's Election as Governor of Minnesota

Stephen I. Frank
Department of Political Science
SCSU Survey
St. Cloud State University

Steven C. Wagner
Department of Political Science
SCSU Survey
St. Cloud State University

Harcourt College Publishers

Fort Worth   Philadelphia   San Diego   New York   Orlando   Austin   San Antonio
Toronto   Montreal   London   Sydney   Tokyo

Custom Publisher: Robert Tessman
Senior Production Manager: Sue Dunaway

"We Shocked the World!"
A Case Study of Jesse Ventura's Election as Governor of Minnesota

This book would not have been possible without the help of several individuals. In particular, the authors would like to thank reviewer Joseph A. Kunkel III, Minnesota State University - Mankato, who read the manuscript and made helpful, critical comments. The text is much improved by his reading. We would also like to thank the print and broadcast journalists, editorialists, and political pundits who monitored and critiqued Ventura's campaign and election. This project would not have been possible without their diligence to inform the public.

Thanks are due also to Bob Tessman of Harcourt Brace who was instrumental in bringing this book to completion. Bob was an invaluable supporter and advocate of this project. Any errors that remain are the authors' alone.

We would especially like to thank our respective partners, Barbara Frank and Karen Lowery Wagner, for their emotional and professional support. The thoughtful feedback Barbara and Karen provided during the writing of this book made it a better product.

Stephen I. Frank
Steven C. Wagner

April, 1999

This book describes the election of Jesse Ventura as Minnesota's thirty-eighth Governor. Initially, almost no one took Jesse Ventura's candidacy seriously. No one thought a former professional wrestler turned gubernatorial candidate for the Reform party had any chance to beat Hubert H. Humphrey III, the Democrat-Farmer-Labor party candidate, or Norman Coleman, the Republican party candidate.

Ventura's campaign was something of a circus side show. He campaigned off the seat of his Harley-Davidson motorcycle, and he had only one paid campaign staff person and a near empty campaign treasury. He was not able to run television advertisements until the end of the campaign. But he had charisma. Humphrey and Coleman ignored candidate Ventura's populist message and sometimes amusing one-liners. They lost the election. Ventura has a sign, a bumper sticker really, hanging above the front door of his private home, and that sign reads, "Forget the Dog. Beware of the Owner." We think Ventura won because Humphrey and Coleman ignored the owner.

This book, which supplements any introductory textbook on American government, state and local government, or parties and elections, shows how and why Ventura won. Our intention is to provide an easy-to-read text that offers insight to a unique gubernatorial campaign. Although the text is a description of Ventura's campaign strategy, we place the election and campaign in the larger context of state politics and governance.

The text opens with an introduction to the structure and nature of Minnesota politics. We show in chapter one that structural characteristics of Minnesota politics allow a populist to successfully seek elective office. Chapter two is a discussion of the parameters of the 1998 Minnesota gubernatorial election. In this chapter we examine the three gubernatorial candidates and how they approached their campaign. Chapter three is a detailed examination of Ventura's campaign strategy and tactics. We show how an underfunded campaign, but a charismatic candidate, is able to win office. Chapter four examines who voted for Ventura and why. Although the chapter is brief, we compare Ventura's vote-getting strategy with exit polling data. In chapter five we ask whether Ventura can govern. Ventura's opportunities to govern are immense but he faces structural constraints, such as a Republican controlled House of Representatives and a Democrat-Farmer-Labor controlled Senate, that may inhibit his governing ability.

"We Shocked the World!"

A Case Study of Jesse Ventura's Election
as Governor of Minnesota

1

Introduction to Minnesota Politics

Political combat does not occur in a vacuum. It occurs in the context of a society's political system (Williamson and Wolsborn, 1998). A political system consists of formal and informal structures and mechanisms that operate to translate or condition societal input into political decisions and actions (Williamson and Wolsborn, 1998). Those who have a stake in political system outcomes create and maintain them for their personal gain. It is common to find challenges to political systems from those who also have a stake in political decisions but believe they lack access to the system. Political systems either adapt to those challenges or wither and die. In American politics, those that have a stake in political decisions, whether previously excluded or not, make their claim though electoral activity.

The political system structures electoral competition. Elections, therefore, reflect the ideas, aspirations, interests, needs, and problems of society (Williamson and Wolsborn, 1998). Minnesota's political system is a reflection of the social, economic, and demographic diversity of the state (Williamson and Wolsborn, 1998). We argue that Minnesota electoral contests and their outcomes also reflect the political and social characteristics of the state. It is because a political system and how it operates is a reflection of society that Jesse Ventura's election, albeit somewhat unlikely, is not a complete surprise.

Daniel Elazar describes Minnesota as a "moralistic" state (1984). Minnesota's cultural orientation to politics considers political activity one of the greatest human activities. Politics is a search for the good society. It is an effort undertaken by politicians and citizens centered on some notion of promoting the public good and a commitment to public welfare. Politicians are honest and selfless. Citizens contribute to political debate and participate in the affairs of governing. We would expect to find competitive political parties, clean but spirited elections, and high voter turnout. The rules that structure political combat should encourage new entrants to the political system. Therefore, it is not surprising to find challenges to dominant political parties from third or minor parties and candidates.

A moralistic political culture compares to "individualistic" and "traditionalistic" cultures. An individualistic state has an orientation toward politics that suggests political activity is "dirty" and the activity of professionals (Elazar, 1984). Politics is not a search for the good society but a reaction to private initiative (Elazar, 1984). We would expect to find strong parties and low voter turnout. Independent or third parties are not encouraged and should have a difficult time making inroads to the voters. Political activity in a traditionalistic state is a means to maintain the existing social order (Elazar, 1984). Politics is a privilege and is enjoyed by the elite (Elazar, 1984). Political parties are centrally organized and highly personal. We expect low voter turnout and structural barriers to the formation of third or independent parties.

An examination of the history of Minnesota politics suggests that it is indeed a moralistic state; because of that, a Jesse Ventura-type candidate has an excellent opportunity to win public office. Minnesota has a history of electing reform-type candidates.

Populists and Progressives

The Republican party dominated northern national politics from 1858 to 1930, but in Minnesota the Republicans dominated until 1950 (Kunkel, 1998). During that time several protest parties and the Democrat party challenged the Republican party. In some respects, the protest parties were stronger than the Democrat party and only when the protest and Democrat party voters formed an alliance were Republican party candidates defeated (Kunkel, 1998). In 1890, for example, a coalition of Farmers' Alliance and Democrat supporters was able to control the state legislature for a single session (Kunkel, 1998). A Republican controlled the governor's office. In 1898 a coalition of Populist and Democrat party supporters elected a governor but the legislature remained in the hands of the Republicans (Kunkel, 1998). The Democrats elected a governor, John A. Johnson, who served from 1904–1910 but the Republican party controlled the legislature (Kunkel, 1998). The Democrat realignment that began to occur early in the 1900s and culminated in Democrat domination nationally in the 1930s slowed in Minnesota largely because the Republican party was fairly progressive (Kunkel, 1998). Voters that may have leaned toward the Democrat party had a potential home in the then progressive Republican party and later on in the Farmer-Labor party.

During this era the progressive factions within the Republican party and the Populists adopted many electoral reforms (Kunkel, 1998). Of particular importance to contemporary Minnesota politics is the direct primary. In an effort to weaken the hold that the conservative majority faction had over the nominating process, progressives successfully sought in 1912 to open the nominating process to the voters (Kunkel, 1998). This would weaken party organization and allow minor factions within a party to capture the party nomination by making an appeal to their supporters in the electorate. Individuals outside the established or majority parties tend to favor the direct primary for one important reason. Interparty contests occasionally leave the party bloodied and weakened, creating an opportunity for minor or third parties to appeal to voters dissatisfied with the outcome of the interparty contest.

Farmer-Labor Challenges to the Republican Party

National politics in the years from 1920 to 1940 were both conservative and radical (Kunkel, 1998). In Minnesota, the Republican party, reeling from the earlier influence of the progressives turned conservative and was able to fend off an attempt by populist and socialist factions to take over the party (Kunkel, 1998). The Minnesota

(Republican) populists attempted to use several of the progressive reforms—direct primaries and nonpartisan legislative elections—in their bid. When it became clear to the populists and socialists in 1918 that they would not dominate the Minnesota Republican party they launched the Farmer-Labor party (Kunkel, 1998). The Democrat party was a third or minor party. The Farmer-Labor party opposed the Republicans.

Although the roots of the Farmer-Labor party are in the progressive movement, the party operated differently from the progressive anti-party ideal. The Farmer-Labor party embraced structured organization, mass membership, and both educational and electoral activities (Kunkel, 1998). Issue articulation was extremely important to the party, as was candidate endorsement. The Farmer-Labor party introduced to Minnesota politics the process of preprimary endorsement, where the party endorses one of its candidates that is competing with other party candidates in the primary (Kunkel, 1998). Preprimary endorsement emulates the pre-Progressive party caucus or convention system of party nominee selection. An interesting outcome of combining preprimary endorsement and an open primary is the possibility the party endorsed candidate may lose the primary.

The Farmer-Labor party experienced many successes in the late 1920s and early 1930s (Kunkel, 1998). These successes were primarily due to its organizational strength and the almost natural appeal of the party to the working class and poor harmed by the Great Depression (Kunkel, 1998). In 1930, the party was able to elect Floyd B. Olson governor (Kunkel, 1998). Unfortunately for the Farmer-Laborites, the Republican conservatives dominated the legislature (Kunkel, 1998). In 1938, Harold E. Stassen, a progressive Republican, defeated Farmer-Laborite Elmer Benson, to capture the governorship. Stassen was able to win primarily because the Farmer-Labor party was breaking into various factions (Kunkel, 1998). Several of the factions, along with the Democratic party, noticed they shared certain similarities: opposition to the Republicans, liberal but not communist, and friendly toward Roosevelt (Kunkel, 1998). In 1944 the Farmer-Labor party and the Democrat party merged and formed the present Democrat-Farmer-Labor party (Kunkel, 1998) .

DFL and Republican Competitiveness

Immediately the Democrat-Farmer-Labor (DFL) party took steps to build unity, purge the more radical elements and gain elective office. One of the early steps, which remains in use today, is the use of preprimary endorsements. Kunkel (1998) argues that the endorsement of Hubert Humphrey led to his election to the U.S. Senate in 1948 and the election of Orville Freeman as governor in 1954. It was also in 1954 that the DFL elected a majority of members to the Minnesota House but not the Senate (Kunkel, 1998). Throughout the 1950s and 1960s, the DFL party and the Republican party were competitive. In the 1960s, however, both parties experienced internal friction. The DFL party split over the war in Vietnam (Kunkel, 1998). A few years later, the Republicans split over the problems associated with Nixon's doomed presidency (Kunkel, 1998). The Minnesota Republican party changed its name to the Independent Republican party from 1975 until 1996 (Kunkel, 1998). This did not help the Republican party retain elected office. The DFL has maintained majorities in the Minnesota House and Senate since the late 1970s and carried every presidential election since 1976 (Kunkel, 1998).

In some respects the Minnesota Republican party remained a liberal or moderate party until the Christian conservatives successfully took control of the party organization in the early 1980s (Kunkel, 1998). This has not generally helped the Republican party gain elected office. The DFL party organization remains committed to its liberal principles. The parties remain well organized but their connection to the voters has weakened. Evidence that suggests a weakening of party-voter connection is abundant.

Growth of Independent Voters

The best single indicator that shows Minnesota's political parties has declined, in terms of voter participation, is the growing number of individuals who see themselves as independent voters. The Minnesota Poll (Kunkel, 1998) reported that about twenty percent of all voters in the mid 1950s saw themselves as independents. The SCSU Survey (1998) reports about forty percent of all Minnesotans see themselves as independent voters today. These voters behave much as one would expect an independent voter to behave: about one-half regularly vote for candidates affiliated with the DFL party or Republican party and the other half does not.

The decline of voter loyalty to the Republican party and (DFL) Democrat party is not limited to Minnesota. The Survey Research Center (1998) reports that nationally, in the middle 1950s, about twenty-two percent of all voters saw themselves as independent. Approximately forty-three percent of the electorate affiliated with the Democrat party and twenty-nine percent identified with the Republican party (Survey Research Center, 1998). In the middle 1990s, however, Democrat party identifiers dropped to thirty-nine percent and Republican party identifiers were stable at twenty-eight percent (Survey Research Center, 1998). The percentage of the electorate that sees themselves as independents had grown to thirty-four percent (Survey Research Center, 1998). Declining loyalty to the parties means that "more members of the electorate are up for grabs each election, and more of them are likely to be swayed by the events, issues and personalities" (Jillson, 1999: 195).

The best example of the strength of independent voters in Minnesota politics is the successes of presidential Reform party candidate Ross Perot. In 1992, Ross Perot captured twenty-four percent of the vote and in 1996 he obtained twelve percent of the popular vote (Minnesota Secretary of State, 1998). Clearly, voters in Minnesota are willing to support a candidate outside the political mainstream. Particularly important for Ventura's candidacy was who voted for Perot. In 1992 and 1996 the disenfranchised middle class voters and young, male suburban voters supported Perot. These voting blocs became important constituencies to Ventura's campaign. Equally important, Minnesota provides financial campaign assistance to candidates of parties that capture five percent of the popular vote. Perot's successes helped qualify Ventura for public funds to assist his campaign.

Campaign Finance

Earlier we pointed out that Minnesota has a moralistic political culture. In states that tend to be moralistic, campaign finance regulation is usually strict. Minnesota is not an exception. In terms of state elections, individuals must limit candidate contributions to two thousand dollars. The same limit applies to political action committees' (PAC) contributions. Individual and organization contributions to political parties are not limited, and political parties may give twenty thousand dollars to their candidates. Candidates have the option of accepting partial public funding of the campaigns. If candidates accepts public funds, they must adhere to spending limits. A candidate's party, however, may freely spend to assist the election of its candidate.

Humphrey and Coleman both agreed to the spending limit of approximately two million dollars. Coleman's share of available public funds was $559,670 and Humphrey's was $603,544 (Minnesota Campaign Finance and Public Disclosure Board, 1999). Ventura also accepted the spending limits and due to past Reform party successes qualified for public assistance, but his share was $308,840 (Minnesota Campaign Finance and Public Disclosure Board, 1999). The campaign receives the allocation after the election if the candidate receives five percent of the vote (Minnesota Campaign Finance and Public Disclosure Board, 1999). Although Ventura received less public money than either Humphrey or Coleman, and he received it after the election, the spending limits imposed on Humphrey and Coleman gave Ventura a fighting chance. See chapter three for a more complete description of Minnesota's gubernatorial campaign finance system.

Primaries and Endorsements

All fifty states use a primary election to nominate some or all statewide candidates. States differ in terms of whether their primary is open to voters who have not previously indicated party affiliation or closed to voters who have not declared party preference. In about thirty percent of the states, parties endorse candidates prior to the primary election. Minnesota now uses a modified closed primary. Voters do not declare party preference prior to the primary but may only vote for candidates of a single party in the primary election. The DFL and Republican parties of Minnesota both endorse their nominee prior to the primary. Candidates not endorsed may run in the primary. The winner of the primary, possibly someone who did not receive the party preprimary endorsement, represents the party in the general election.

Party preprimary endorsement does not guarantee candidate success in the primary. Attendance is low at the Minnesota Republican party endorsing convention and the DFL Party endorsement caucus, and those that attend are often strong party activists. For the Republican party, this has often meant that the most conservative candidate obtains the preprimary endorsement, and for the DLFers, the most liberal candidate is often endorsed. If a candidate does not connect with these factions they have no chance of becoming the party nominee. If selected, the nominee may have difficulty winning the general election. In Minnesota and elsewhere, most voters are moderate (SCSU Survey, 1998). This complex process could alienate the voters if the moderates feel both candidates are too extreme.

Norm Coleman won his party's preprimary endorsement after several ballots. The candidates that unsuccessfully sought the Republican endorsement agreed they would not contest Coleman in the primary. Humphrey did not obtain the DLF party endorsement. Yet, he easily won his contested primary. Many voters saw the endorsement process and the primary contest as a "game" of the party activists, to the exclusion of the voters. We suggest that Ventura was able to capitalize on the dissatisfaction of the voters with the Republican and DFL endorsement and primary process and made a successful appeal to them. We find this particularly interesting because Coleman and Humphrey were the more moderate among their parties' candidates. At times, however, it was difficult to determine the ideological positions of Humphrey and Coleman.

Voter Participation

If there is one politically oriented activity that is easy to do in Minnesota it is voting. State law has made registration easy and voting simple. The SCSU Survey (1998) reports eighty-five percent of eligible voters are registered to vote and, for a presidential election, turnout averages sixty-five percent. Turnout for Ventura's election was sixty-one percent, the highest in the nation for a non-presidential election year. In order to vote in Minnesota, one must meet several basic eligibility guidelines. The Minnesota voter eligibility guidelines are contained in Box 1.

Voting is so easy that persons in jail for a misdemeanor may vote by absentee ballot. Access to an absentee ballot is possible for any reason. The political parties make regular practice of mailing absentee ballots to likely voters, even if they have not requested such a ballot. The state Republican party mailed two hundred fifty thousand absentee ballots for the general election to likely Coleman voters.

Voting is easy and turnout high because registration is easy. Indeed, one must register to vote, but state law makes registration a painless process. Minnesotans may register to vote by mail or in person up to twenty days before an election. Candidates and parties may go door-to-door with voter applications and even help people fill out the forms (Backstrom, 1998). Minnesotans may register when they apply for their drivers license or pay annual income taxes. In the case of college students, they may register when they pay their tuition (Backstrom, 1998). Finally, Minnesota allows potential voters to register to vote at the polls on election day. The potential voter will need identification to show they live in the

---

BOX 1   **MINNESOTA VOTER ELIGIBILITY GUIDELINES**

- Be a United States citizen
- Attained age eighteen
- Lived for 20 days in the voting precinct
- Have not been convicted of a felony (although one may after conviction have voting rights restored)
- Not live under guardianship or have been judged mentally incompetent

precinct or have someone vouch for them. In the 1996 presidential election and the 1998 gubernatorial election, approximately fifteen percent of the voters registered on election day (Backstrom, 1998, and Minnesota Office of the Secretary of State, 1999). Exit polling (discussed in chapter four) suggests that one of the reasons Ventura won was the high number of new voters who were young and overwhelmingly voted for him.

Discussion Questions

1. Compare and contrast moralistic political culture with individualist and traditionalistic political cultures and how they might differently influence the structure of state government and state politics.

2. Define party competitiveness. How does Minnesota (or any state) compare with other states?

3. Compare Minnesota electoral finance guidelines with other states. How does Minnesota differ in its approach to publicly financed gubernatorial campaigns and the U.S. presidential campaign?

4. Compare and contrast Minnesota voter registration guidelines with other states. Do registration guidelines influence turnout?

References

Backstrom, Charles H. 1998. "Conducting Elections in Minnesota." In Steve Hoffman, Donald Ostrom, Homer Williamson and Kay Wolsborn, eds. *Perspectives on Minnesota Government and Politics*. 4th Edition. Edina, MN: Burgess Publishing. Pp. 219–250.

Elazar, Daniel J. 1984. *American Federalism: A View From The States*. 3rd Edition. New York: Harper and Row, Publishers.

Jillson, Cal. 1999. *American Government: Political Change and Institutional Development*. Fort Worth, TX: Harcourt Brace College Publishers.

Kunkel III, Joseph A. 1998. "Political Parties in Minnesota." In Steve Hoffman, Donald Ostrom, Homer Williamson and Kay Wolsborn, eds. *Perspectives on Minnesota Government and Politics*. 4th Edition. Edina, MN: Burgess Publishing. Pp. 161–188.

Minnesota Campaign Finance and Public Disclosure Board. 1999. *Candidate Filings*. State of Minnesota.

Minnesota Office of the Secretary of State. 1998. *Official General Election Vote Totals by County for Office of Governor, 1998*. State of Minnesota.

SCSU Survey. 1998. *Annual Statewide Omnibus Survey*. St. Cloud State University, St. Cloud, MN.

Survey Research Center. 1998. Center for Political Studies, *National Election Studies*. Inter-Universtiy Consortium for Political and Social Research. University of Michigan, Ann Arbor, MI.

Williamson, Homer E. and Kay Wolsborn. 1998. "Introduction." In Steve Hoffman, Donald Ostrom, Homer Williamson and Kay Wolsborn, eds. *Perspectives on Minnesota Government and Politics*. 4th Edition. Edina, MN: Burgess Publishing. Pp. 5–8.

2

Parameters of the 1998 Gubernatorial Election

It is impossible to identify one factor that led to Jesse Ventura's candidacy. Instead, we argue that several factors and events led to Ventura's decision to enter the gubernatorial contest. It is the convergence of these factors and events that also assisted greatly in Ventura's win.

Structural Factors

Two factors, growth of independent voters in Minnesota and electoral inroads of Reform party candidates, combined to lay the foundation for Ventura's success. Approximately forty percent of Minnesota voters do not claim affiliation with either the Republican party or DFL party. Nonetheless, only twelve to seventeen percent are "true" independents and the majority (about twenty-eight to twenty-three percent) vote for either the Republican or DFL party candidates. The independent voters, however, have shown a recent history of voting for Reform party candidates. As noted in chapter one, Perot was able to capture many of these voters in his two bids for the presidency.

In terms of Minnesota statewide elections, Dean Barkely ran as a Reform party candidate for the Sixth congressional district in 1992 and for the senate in both 1994 and 1996. Although Barkley did not win these races, he captured enough votes (1992: 17% of the vote; 1994: 5% of the vote; 1996: 7% of the vote) to obtain "major party status" by the Minnesota Campaign Finance and Public Disclosure Board. This opened the door for a Reform party candidate for governor to receive public funding. Later on, public funding allowed Ventura to air radio and television advertisements. Without public funds, the campaign could not have run the advertisements and it is doubtful that Ventura would have won. Almost one-half of Ventura's campaign budget consisted of public funds (Minnesota Campaign Finance and Public Disclosure Board, 1999).

Equally important to the growth of independent voters and publicly financed campaigns is Minnesota's same day registration law. As noted in chapter one, Minnesota allows eligible voters to register to vote on election day. An important linchpin in Ventura's gubernatorial campaign strategy was the ability of candidate Ventura to excite newly eligible and alienated voters to register and vote. Ventura had previously shown his ability to capture new voters. In 1990 when he ran and won the Brooklyn Park mayoral race his election was due to the turnout of new voters. Approximately 20,000 voted in that election. This compares to the 2,600 votes cast in 1987 Brooklyn Park municipal elections.

Republican and DFL Candidates

Ventura should not have had a chance to win the election. Although the independent voter bloc is large and public funds for the campaign were available, the Republican party and the DFL party nominated what initially seemed excellent candidates. As it turned out, however, both candidates were rather bland, committed several tactical errors and eventually became "straight men" for Ventura's populist (and often outrageous) campaign.

The Republican party nominated St. Paul's incumbent mayor, Norman Coleman. We noted in chapter one that the Republican and DFL parties use a long and cumbersome process to pick their nominees. Coleman was first required to obtain state convention supporters at precinct party caucuses. Although challenged by Lieutenant Governor Joanne Benson, state senator Roy Terwillegar, and Allen Quist, Coleman was successful at this task. His success was largely due to his acceptance of many conservative policies.

The active grass roots members of the Republican party generally comprise the most conservative faction of the state Republicans. Coleman, in order to obtain their support, embraced the policy positions of this faction of the party. Coleman's financial resources were abundant and he received support from notable Republicans: incumbent Republican Governor Arnie Carlson, Member of Congress Jim Ramstad, Minnesota House Minority Leader (currently Speaker) Steve Swiggum, and former Representative Vin Weber. Although Coleman once was a DLFer and initially elected as St. Paul's mayor as a DFL candidate, he had switched to the Republican party (three years earlier) and quickly adopted pragmatic, conservative policies. The state Republican party endorsed his candidacy at their June state convention and he easily won the September 15 primary. At the same time, it is important to point out that the more staunch and conservative Republicans did not completely trust Coleman. These individuals tended to see Coleman as an east coast liberal, former Humphrey employee, Wellstone supporter, and recent convert to the Republican party. We suggest that Coleman was a "wounded" candidate at the beginning of the general election campaign. Box 2 contains a biographical sketch of Mayor Coleman.

The winner of the DFL party primary was Hubert H. Humphrey III. The DFL Party nomination process was much more interesting than the Republican party process. Five prominent DFLers sought to represent their party in the election. Many media observers dubbed the contest the race of the "three sons."

BOX 2	BIOGRAPHY: NORMAN COLEMAN
Born:	Brooklyn, New York, August 17, 1949
Education:	BA, Hofstra University; JD, University of Iowa
Current/Previous Occupations:	Mayor, St. Paul, Minnesota; Solicitor General, Chief Prosecutor, Office of Attorney General, State of Minnesota
Marital Status:	Married, Two Children
Home:	St. Paul, Minnesota
Party Affiliation:	Republican

Humphrey's father served as Mayor of Minneapolis, U.S. Senator, vice president, and unsuccessfully sought the presidency in 1968. Mike Freeman, whose father served as Governor of Minnesota and was in President John F. Kennedy's cabinet, challenged Humphrey. The third "son" was Ted Mondale, whose father also served in the U.S. Senate, was vice president for Jimmy Carter, and also unsuccessfully sought the presidency. Mondale had the support of suburban moderate DFLers. The fourth candidate was Mark Dayton, of Dayton's department store fame. Dayton had previously sought an open Senate seat but was unsuccessful. Finally, state senator Doug Johnson made a respectful bid for the nomination. Johnson ran a cleaver campaign, attacking the "three sons" and Dayton as too rich, but he seemed out of touch with the party's social liberal factions. The only candidate that took the precinct caucuses seriously and sought county delegates to the party endorsement convention was Mike Freeman. He also had backing of the AFL-CIO and U.S. Senator Wellstone. He easily captured the party endorsement at the June convention. All five candidates campaigned during the primary.

Although Mike Freeman was the party's endorsee, Humphrey easily won the nomination with thirty-seven percent of the primary vote. Humphrey had obvious name recognition and had served the state for the past sixteen years as attorney general. As a champion of Minnesota consumers, Humphrey had just won a six billion dollar settlement from the tobacco companies. Overall, Humphrey was a pragmatic liberal. He previously opposed elective abortion services but prior to the election became pro-choice. It is important to note Humphrey was out of campaign funds at the conclusion of the primary. This opened the door to about two weeks of unanswered attack advertisements run by Coleman. We suggest this put Humphrey on the defensive at the beginning of the general election campaign and he was unable to initiate an offensive strategy. Box 3 contains a brief biographical sketch of Humphrey.

The Republican party nominated a pragmatic conservative. The DFL Party nominated a pragmatic liberal. The two parties saw their candidates as "safe bets." Coleman could easily appeal to conservative Minnesotans, and Humphrey, with probably the premier name, could easily appeal to liberal Minnesotans. Although this did create a bipolar ideologically based contest, the two parties felt safe since most indicators suggested voters would support the status quo.

BOX 3	BIOGRAPHY: HUBERT H. HUMPHREY, III
Born:	Minneapolis, Minnesota, June 26, 1942
Education:	BA, American University; JD, University of Minnesota
Previous Occupations:	Attorney General, State of Minnesota; Minnesota State Senator; Private Law Practice
Marital Status:	Married, Three Children
Home:	Minnesota
Party Affiliation:	Democrat-Farmer-Labor

Current Political, Economic, and Social Indicators

Political, economic, and social indicators often factor heavily into an election. As a rule, if the economy is growing, crime is low, and the governmental apparatus is efficient and effective most voters will support the status quo and keep the incumbent person or party in office. An examination of Minnesota on various socioeconomic indicators suggests the 1998 gubernatorial election would support the status quo. In other words, either Coleman or Humphrey should have won the election because there was not a pressing issue, the state was generating huge surpluses, and both were apparently strong candidates. Although neither candidate was the incumbent governor, Humphrey was the incumbent Attorney General and Coleman was (is) the Mayor of St. Paul.

In the greater Twin Cities area, unemployment is at a historic low of about one and one-half percent (Minnesota Department of Employment Security, 1999). Two of the state's other metropolitan areas—St. Cloud and Rochester—enjoy similarly low unemployment (Minnesota Department of Employment Security, 1999). The Duluth metropolitan area has not been as fortunate and has continued to experience higher levels of unemployment. (Minnesota Department of Employment Security, 1999). The level of unemployment in several "out-state" areas, particularly in the north, is also higher than the Twin Cities, St. Cloud, and Rochester metropolitan areas (Minnesota Department of Employment Security, 1999). Overall, the state's unemployment is about two and one-half to three percent (Minnesota Department of Employment Security, 1999). This compares favorably to the four and one-half percent unemployment in the nation.

The record level of unemployment has influenced the level of home ownership. Inversely related to unemployment, the rate of home ownership is at an all time high throughout most of the state (Multiple Listing Service, 1999). Further, the market value of resale homes has dramatically increased and new home construction is strong (Multiple Listing Service, 1999).

Throughout the state, crime rates have declined (Minnesota Department of Public Safety, 1999). This might be the result of low unemployment and rising incomes. Regardless of the cause, crime has decreased. Historically, crime is a major campaign issue and candidates on the wrong side of "crime and punishment" are usually defeated. In this election, crime was not a particularly important issue. The SCSU Survey (1998) found that very few individuals (two percent) surveyed prior to the election rated candidate position on crime as an important reason to vote for one of the three candidates.

At the same time, student test scores are up (Minnesota Department of Children, Families and Learning, 1999). Minnesota has always invested in its public school system. Indeed, class size has increased in elementary schools, but high school students are doing better on college entrance examinations than in the past (Minnesota Department of Children, Families and Learning, 1999).

All indications suggest that the state government is operating efficiently and effectively. State political leaders show a willingness to listen to the public. Throughout 1997 and into 1998, the owner of the Minnesota Twins baseball team sought a new, publicly funded stadium. The voters clearly indicated to their state elected officials that they did not want their taxes used to finance a new baseball stadium. Although several proposals circulated through the legislature during the 1998 session, not a single one received serious attention.

If there was one issue that voters focused on, it was the growing tax surplus. Record levels of unemployment and increasing wages have resulted in growing state revenue surpluses. The legislature enacted a modest proposal to rebate property taxes to the voters. The majority of the surplus is due to higher than expected income tax and sales tax revenue. In 1998, the legislature financed various capital projects with the surplus. The surplus was a major factor in Ventura's decision to run for governor and was an important campaign issue. Ventura said that he would, upon taking office, give back the surplus. Unknown to him, the surplus was previously committed to a modest property tax rebate and several capital projects by the legislature.

In summary, issues that might lead voters to seek a major change in government through their ability to vote were absent. This led most media and academic observers to conclude the election would support the status quo. Thus, either Coleman or Humphrey would win. This conclusion was wrong. The strong socioeconomic indicators seem to have created an environment where voters were willing to take a chance on a candidate that did not represent the status quo.

Candidate Jesse Ventura

Jesse Ventura sought the mayor's position in Brooklyn Park because he disagreed with proposed zoning changes across the street from his home. He argued that the established politicians were not listening to the voters and enacting policy based on their private agendas. Ventura entered the gubernatorial race because he thought the tax surplus belonged to the voters. He also found the established political forces were either too conservative or too liberal. According to Ventura, the bipolar Republican and DFL parties had forgotten the more moderate voters like himself. He saw himself as a regular "working stiff" whom entrenched politicians no longer recognized. Further, he argued that a plurality of Minnesotans shared his fiscal conservative and social liberal views.

Ventura is a self-defined "libertarian." His philosophical approach to the role of government places individual liberty and free choice in a cherished position. According to Ventura, government is limited and evaluated in how well it is noninterventionist in the lives of ordinary citizens. During the campaign, it became clear Ventura shares libertarian ideas. He argued against government regulation and increasing taxes, and he supports free choice. At the same time, Ventura is clearly not a pure libertarian. He does not support governmental assistance to parents of school aged children to attend private schools. Instead, he supports increasing the effectiveness of public schools.

Additionally, Ventura is a "populist." He is a reformer of the establishment and an adherent of "good government." Perhaps this is where we find the basis of his support of better public schools and elimination of all plans for a state school voucher program. He promotes open political participation and shuns special interest control of governmental processes. In large part, he was elected because it is easy for Minnesotans to participate in state electoral activity. Throughout the campaign, he refused to accept donations from political action committees and lobbyists and attacked their role in government.

An important factor of Ventura's candidacy was his past history of working with the Reform party. While hosting a local radio talk show (KFAN), Ventura often had Dean Barkley on and they talked about a wide range of issues and the importance of an alternative party in Minnesota. Although Barkley was unsuccessful at his elective office bids, he was able to established a working friendship with Ventura. He found that Ventura shared his view that the Republican and DFL parties were too ideological and too entrenched.

Barkley also recognized that Ventura possessed many characteristics needed for a successful gubernatorial campaign. These included high name recognition and an innate ability to speak honestly. Ventura also had charisma. In Barkley's 1996 Senate bid Ventura served as his campaign manager. Barkley noticed that at campaign functions Ventura received more attention than he did. Barkley also recognized that Ventura had little to lose. Therefore, Ventura could campaign against the career politicians that he seemed to hold in contempt. He had various ideas about the nature of government that had an appeal; that is, they did not seem canned and came from Ventura's heart.

Ventura is an entertainer. Thus, he was able to approach the campaign as an entertainer while Humphrey and Coleman played a traditional game of politics. Kunkel (1999) suggests that Ventura's candidacy, although an unlikely potential winner, fits into an increasing trend in American politics. As parties weaken and media becomes more pervasive the field is wide open for entertainers to break into politics and redefine the rules (Kunkel, 1999). This is not the first time, nor probably the last, that an entertainer ran successfully for office. Ronald Reagan was an actor, an entertainer, when elected Governor of California. Reagan was ridiculed for not having political and policy skills but his opponents constantly underrated him (Kunkel, 1999). Ventura is even more of an outsider, lacking party or well-developed ideology, advisers, or even the political background that Reagan had (Kunkel, 1999). We suggest this is one of the many keys to Ventura's success.

Ventura was clearly aware of the potential his entertainer and celebrity status held for his candidacy, and he "milked" that status. Ventura approached the campaign as the heir to Howard Beal in *Network* who shouts "I'm mad as hell and I'm not going to take it any more." Ventura had the ability to tap into the "motherload" of popular culture, jump across the boundary from entertainment to politics, and persuade enough voters that they had nothing to lose by electing him (Kunkel, 1999).

Finally, it was clear that Ventura would stand out from the Republican and DFL candidates. Ventura has a distinct voice, a shaved head, and is six feet, four inches tall, weighing approximately 250 pounds. Box 4 contains a brief biographical sketch of Ventura.

BOX 4	BIOGRAPHY: JESSE VENTURA

Born:	James George Janos, Minneapolis, Minnesota, June 15, 1951
Education:	Attended North Hennepin Community College
Previous Occupations:	Radio Talk Show Host; Actor; Mayor, Brooklyn Park, Minnesota; Professional Sports Announcer; Professional Wrestler; Member, Mongols, California Motorcycle Club; Navy SEAL
Marital Status:	Married, Two Children
Home:	Maple Grove, Minnesota
Party Affiliation:	Reform

In August 1997, Ventura informally announced his intention to run for Governor of Minnesota as the Reform party candidate. Dean Barkley was confident Ventura could win if the Republican and DFL parties nominated pro-life candidates (Ventura is pro-choice). He also knew that advertising was necessary and would cost five hundred thousand dollars. Barkley knew that Ventura must excite young, new voters to support his candidacy. Barkley also knew that if the candidates debated and Ventura participated, he would win.

At first, Ventura dragged his feet and only talked about his candidacy and failed to raise campaign revenues. It was not until January 1998 that Ventura formally announced his candidacy. In June, the Reform party held its statewide convention and selected Ventura as its gubernatorial candidate. Barkley immediately sent Ventura to participate in summer parades and other public events. The idea was for Ventura to develop his ideas and a campaign persona. On July 21, Ventura formally filed as a candidate. Ventura ran unopposed in the September 15 primary. At that point, Ventura's successful campaign to become Minnesota's thirty-eighth Governor began.

Discussion Questions

1. Was there anything in the background of the three candidates that indicated one should easily win and others should lose?

2. How did same day registration and publicly funded campaigns provide a structural environment for Ventura's successful candidacy? Was there anything about Ventura, the person, that was necessary for the structural factors to aid in his election?

3. How is it possible for someone who is profane and relished the image of the "Terminator" win an election in a state that is described as "Minnesota Nice?"

4. If you are interested in learning more about libertarianism, we suggest you visit the Janda, Berr, and Goldman "idealog" Web site, at http:www.hmco.com/college/COD/home.html.

References

Kunkel III, Joseph A. 1999. Correspondence to the Authors.

Minnesota Campaign Finance and Public Disclosure Board. 1999. *Candidate Filings*. State of Minnesota.

Minnesota Department of Children, Families and Learning. 1999. *District School Profiles*. State of Minnesota.

Minnesota Department of Employment Security. 1999. *Minnesota Unemployment Statistics*. State of Minnesota.

Minnesota Department of Public Safety. 1999. *Minnesota Crime Information–1997*. State of Minnesota.

Multiple Listing Service. 1999. Minnesota Association of Realtors. St. Paul, MN.

SCSU Survey. 1998. *Annual General Purpose Statewide Survey*. St. Cloud State University.

3

Ventura's Campaign

Jesse Ventura won the governor's race in part because his opposition consisted of two cautious and slightly wounded candidates. Coleman and Humphrey helped Ventura's candidacy when they accepted public funds to finance their campaigns. This limited the amount they spent on their campaigns. Ventura also received public funds; however, he received about one-half the amount Coleman and Humphrey received. Nonetheless, this helped equalize the race in terms of campaign finances. We argue the race lacked an issue or issues that normally galvanize voters to support a seasoned political veteran. Therefore, Ventura was able to campaign on his personality.

Campaign Strategy, Issues, and Debates

Ventura's campaign strategy was rather simple. Early in the campaign his advisers decided to seek free publicity and make heavy use of the Internet. The campaign targeted the greater Twin Cities area. Approximately one-half of all eligible voters reside in the Twin Cities area. Also, the major Twin Cities media outlets reach about eighty percent of the state. Ventura emphasized "style" over "substance" that perfectly fit the Ventura persona. Finally, Ventura's success hinged on his ability to attract young voters new to politics and alienated middle-class voters.

Ventura's primary campaign advisers consisted of two individuals. Dean Barkley served as campaign chairperson and chief strategist. Barkley joined the Reform party in the early 1990s and, as previously stated, unsuccessfully sought elected office as a Reform candidate three separate times. Barkley is a lawyer and at the outset of the campaign was operating a car wash in the suburb of Golden Valley. The second key campaign adviser was another Reform party supporter, Doug Friedline, who served as campaign manager. He also joined the Reform Party in the early 1990s and worked for Perot's 1992 campaign and Barkley's 1994 and 1996 Senate bids. Friedline operates a "pull tab" operation in a suburban Ramsey bar.

Two additional Reform party members handled communications. Key to assuring Ventura's message was readily available was the responsibility of Phil Madson, who relied on the Internet. Madson founded the Reform party in Minnesota and served as organizer for Perot's 1992 Minnesota presidential campaign. At the outset of the campaign, Madson was a self employed computer consultant in suburban Lino Lakes.

Madson served as campaign treasurer. Finally, Geraldine Drewry was in charge of news releases and answered media questions. Drewry operates a public relations firm from her home. The campaign did not have a pollster and was not able to employ a radio and television consultant until the end of September.

Ventura campaigned as a classic outsider. Initially, it appeared Ventura could not possibly win the election. Polling data from a statewide survey taken after the September 15 primary showed Humphrey with a substantial lead. Of likely voters (defined as those who voted recently and were either registered or planning to register and vote), approximately fifty percent indicated a commitment to voting for Humphrey (Minnesota Poll, 1998). Norm Coleman had the support of twenty-nine percent and Ventura had a lock on only ten percent (Minnesota Poll, 1998).

A candidate outside the major parties, with no apparent chance of winning, has extraordinary latitude with the voters, other candidates, and media. Ventura took full advantage of this opportunity. In many respects this was easy given Ventura's persona. Ventura campaigned as an outsider. He was irrepressible and outrageous. He was often loud, confrontational, and brash. As an entertainer, Ventura made heavy use of props—his military experience, leather coats, and his body. Without a doubt, Ventura provided voters with a candidate that contrasted with "politics as usual." More than anything else, this attracted the youth vote.

A key element to Ventura success was obtaining the middle class, moderate voters. As it turned out, Ventura was immediately able to connect to the middle class. He argued that he would represent the average taxpayer because he was an average taxpayer. It is noteworthy that Ventura's estimated income throughout the 1990s is about two million dollars. Nonetheless, the middle class bought the act. Humphrey thought he would ride into office on the middle class vote. The state's largest labor union supporting Humphrey, AFL-CIO, found that it was reaching more Ventura supporters with its "get-out-the-vote" telephone callers than committed Humphrey voters near the end of October.

Reaching the middle class, who seemed unsatisfied with Humphrey and Coleman, proved easy for Ventura. At campaign events, Ventura spoke with candor and compassion. He offered an anti-establishment message that voters sought. His talk was plain and he suggested his style of governing would be "hands-on." At the same time, he confessed his lack of knowledge about the details of running the state and said he would rely on his agency commissioners (cabinet) to run government.

He railed against bureaucrats and government in general. One of his slogans was "Retaliate in '98." This is an unusual slogan given low unemployment, budget surpluses, and diminishing crime rates. Nonetheless, the slogan found its mark among voters that seemed bored with politicians who campaign and govern by focus groups and polls.

Although Ventura's issue positions seemed to come from personal gripes, they found a mark among the middle class. He argued that Minnesotans paid too much for personal vehicle registration, pointing out that in Wisconsin vehicle tags cost about fifty dollars per year whereas Minnesotans might pay several hundred. Ventura questioned the annual fee for personal watercraft. He attacked the very existence of the High Occupancy Commuter Lanes in the Twin Cities. A casual reading of newspaper letters to the editors suggests that no one, except perhaps transportation planners, likes the commuter lanes.

Finally, Ventura attacked taxes, the bane of the middle classes. Completely lacking any details, Ventura suggested that property taxes be frozen, property tax assessors eliminated, and previous state budget surpluses returned. He also said that not a single tax dime is appropriate to finance professional sports stadiums. About one year before the election, many elected officials, contrary to voter wishes, tried to assemble a financial package to build a new baseball stadium for the Twins. As it turned out, they were unable to put a package together.

What we find interesting about Ventura's issue positions is how well they correspond to his libertarian philosophy and brought voters, especially youth and females, to his campaign. Ventura's campaign style and his policy positions showed he understood the importance of pop culture to attract young voters. A typical campaign event had Ventura quoting late rock-and-roll singers Jim Morrison and Jerry Garcia. Ventura poked fun at DFLer Humphrey and Republican Coleman by comparing them with biker clubs, the "ReBLOODicans" and "DemoCRYPTS." He argued that Coleman and Humphrey were too much a part of politics as usual and offered nothing to young voters. Ventura unabashedly told crowds that he supported gay rights and public school education. One of his appeals to youthful voters, which also connected with others, was his position on gun control. Ventura suggested that gun control, by government, was simply wrong. He further stated that the only gun control that he recognized was the "ability to put two rounds in the same spot." Humor or libertarian principles? The voters did not seem to care. They liked his "attitude."

One of the problems Ventura faced early in the campaign was the "gender gap." It was clear that males easily related to Ventura. Ventura's persona as a "bad boy" former professional wrestler that had a fondness for personal watercraft and motorcycles fit nicely with his appeal to males. However, Ventura's advisers expressed some concern that this persona may work against attracting female voters. Early in the campaign, Ventura chose as his running mate Mae Schunk, a 64-year-old public school teacher. Later in the campaign, when questioned about his support for public schools, Ventura said that a priority would be the reduction in class size. He further noted that all other school policy would be the responsibility of Mae Schrunk, "A 64 year old schoolmarm." Ventura mixed a little humor with his notion that educators, not St. Paul bureaucrats, should be instrumental in policy making.

Norm Coleman embraced the Republican party position that elective abortion procedures are wrong. Humphrey's position on abortion had changed from pro-life to pro-choice. Ventura stated unequivocally that he is pro-choice. This position cost him some votes, but it also brought him many more supporters, especially females. Two actions—picking Mae Schunck as his running mate and his position on abortion—closed the "gender gap."

If there is a single, identifiable turning point in the campaign it came when Humphrey insisted he would not debate Coleman without also including Ventura. Humphrey thought it was a stroke of genius. Instead, it was a major error. He incorrectly thought that if Ventura appeared raw and uninformed the voters would stay with a safe, professional politician. Humphrey also mistakenly thought that Ventura would take votes away from Coleman. In the 1992 presidential campaign, Perot took votes from Republican President Bush, helping Democrat challenger Clinton win the election (Lowi and Ginsberg, 1994). Thus, Humphrey followed the Clinton strategy by focusing on economic conservatism. He thought this would attract independents and Reagan Democrats. As it turned out, the strategy failed. Ventura's socially tolerant "attitude" attracted Humphrey supporters and perhaps moderate Republicans. Later in the campaign when it became apparent to both Humphrey and Coleman that Ventura had a real chance of winning, neither Humphrey nor Coleman knew what to do. Coleman tried to get a negative message out about Ventura but it failed. Humphrey did nothing.

All three candidates participated in a total of nine debates. Three received statewide coverage. Normally debates reinforce existing attitudes and opinions of likely voters. However, the large number of debates attracted an unusual amount of attention and was better than average broadcast and print media coverage. The amount of attention paid the debates were the result of three mediating factors. One, there was not an incumbent governor. Incumbents have an unusually high chance of reelection. Thus, all three candidates appeared as likely winners of the debates and the election. Second, the tracking polls suggested that likely voters were fluid in terms of which candidate they intended to support. Thus, voters were more attentive to the debates as a source of information about the candidates. Third, Jesse Ventura was an unknown commodity that Humphrey insisted be included in the debates. Thus, the media and the voters paid attention to the debates to see the show Ventura was likely to offer.

The first debate, which received statewide television and radio coverage, was in Brainard, a small northern community. Humphrey and Coleman needed to do well in this debate. Historically, northern Minnesota votes heavily DFL. Humphrey merely needed to appear knowledgeable and articulate regarding standard DFL policy positions. At the same time, Coleman recognized he could capture many of these voters if he appeared moderate and appealed to the agricultural base.

Throughout the evening, Humphrey conveyed the image of a decent individual who lacked imagination and personality. Coleman also appeared to be a decent individual but also a fiscal and social conservative. Coleman's issue positions showed that he lacked consistency. Humphrey pointed out that Coleman was a one time college protester (Humphrey ran television advertisements to reinforce the image) and also served as chairperson of Senator Wellstone's first Senate campaign. Wellstone is the last true liberal in the senate.

As Humphrey and Coleman fought over policy positions and ideology, Ventura asserted that his campaign is about rejection of politics as usual. Ventura quickly became the star. He was funny and proved to be a plain speaker of personal or homespun wisdom. Indeed, he appeared raw and often uninformed. He conveyed a certain pride in not knowing policy details. His ignorance became an asset and helped to immediately connect with the voters, who often do not know minute details of tax and spending policies. Ventura seemed to be a mirror image of the voters.

Humphrey, accused by Coleman of being a typical "tax and spend" liberal, promised to not raise taxes. Coleman tried to further repair an error he previously committed. At one point, Coleman suggested the family farm was in need of redefinition for the next Century. To show the voters he was not out of touch with Minnesota farmers he called for farm subsidies and a cut in property taxes. Ventura attacked both for lacking leadership skills and partisan bickering. Humphrey and Coleman, thinking the battle was between them, smiled. The St. Paul *Pioneer Press* reported that while Coleman and Humphrey battled, Ventura charmed the crowd.

Coleman and Humphrey fared no better at the second statewide debate, held October 6 in Hibbing. Again, Humphrey believed this debate would assure him of victory. Hibbing is a northern community that historically has strongly supported DFL candidates. Coleman also thought he would come out of this debate a winner. In an attempt to repair his image after his comments about the need to redefine the family farm he spent many days campaigning in rural areas. Coleman saw the debate as a chance to further clarify his family farm comment and solidify his support in the north. Humphrey and Coleman were both wrong. They also committed an error by not attacking Ventura because they thought he would fade and both could then capture his supporters. They accepted the "wasted vote theory" that suggests independent candidate supporters will eventually vote for main party candidates once they realize their candidate can not win. Similar to the first debate, Humphrey and Coleman fought and Ventura used his theatrical skills to please the crowd.

The third statewide debate, held October 11, ended Humphrey and Coleman's chance of beating Ventura. Once again, Humphrey and Coleman fought. Humphrey charged Coleman with putting the city of St. Paul deeply in debt to pay for construction of a professional hockey team stadium. Coleman called Humphrey a spendthrift, noting the Attorneys General's Office budget skyrocketed while Humphrey served as attorney general. Coleman accused Humphrey of lying about his record and eventually filed suit in eighty-seven Minnesota counties charging Humphrey with breaking the State Fair Campaign Practices Act for lying. Ventura appeared, once again, above the battle. To show his compassion he endorsed gay rights, noting that "love is bigger than government."

The Minnesota Poll (1998) tracked voter support of the three candidates throughout the campaign, and in October reported that Ventura had climbed to twenty-one percent. Humphrey's support had dropped from fifty-three percent in September to thirty-five (Minnesota Poll, 1998). Coleman was at thirty-four percent (Minnesota Poll, 1998). Ventura's advisers became confident that their candidate had a real chance of winning. They also knew that television advertisements would be necessary if he was going to climb any further and win.

At this point, Coleman and Humphrey realized Ventura had a chance of beating them. Also, the media recognized that Ventura could possibly win the election. Humphrey and Coleman did nothing to stop the rapid movement of their supporters to Ventura. Instead, they continued to attack each other. This fed Ventura's assertion that Humphrey and Coleman continued to represent politics as usual.

The media gave Ventura a free ride—they failed to make Ventura provide details about his policy pronouncements. Once a reporter asked Ventura how he might work with a legislature that lacks Reform Party members to help assure legislative success. Ventura responded by rolling up his sleeve and flexing a biceps muscle and telling the reporter, "That's how." The voters simply went wild.

Equally important to Ventura's campaign at this time was a loan made by Franklin National Bank, used to finance television advertisements. The importance of television advertisements to Ventura's campaign is impossible to estimate. Therefore, this subject receives greater attention later in the chapter.

A major concern of Ventura's advisers was whether or not his supporters would shift to Humphrey or Coleman in the final days of the campaign. They thought that if Ventura could climb to approximately thirty percent in the tracking polls, Ventura's supporters would remain committed to Ventura. On October 31, the SCSU Survey released its statewide assessment of what Minnesota voters were likely to do on election day (1998). The Survey found that voters felt slightly "warmer" toward Ventura than to either Coleman or Humphrey. The respondents rated the candidates on a "feeling thermometer," that ranged from zero, which equaled cold, to one hundred, which equaled very hot. Ventura received a fifty-four, while Coleman received fifty-three, and Humphrey received a fifty-one (SCSU Survey, 1998). This shows the voters had not only "warmed up" to Ventura's candidacy but were not going to defect from Ventura to Humphrey or Coleman.

The SCSU Survey (1998) also inquired whom the respondents were leaning toward supporting on election day. Humphrey and Coleman tied at thirty-two percent and Ventura had the committed support of twenty-seven percent of likely voters. The margin of error in the survey was plus or minus four percent. The SCSU Survey (1998) concluded the race was too close to call. Ventura's supporters had not defected to Humphrey or Coleman.

The SCSU Survey (1998) asked the respondents why they were planning to vote for the candidate of their choice. Table 1 shows that Coleman and Humphrey received the support of those that focused on public policies. Those voters that intended to support a candidate because of personal characteristics clearly favored Ventura.

The final major activity that aided Ventura's win was a seventy-two hour recreational tour of Minnesota, dubbed the "Drive to Victory Tour." In many respects this was a "get out the vote" effort. Ventura's advisers knew he could not win without high voter turnout. If they could stage an event that obtained media attention and grass roots support, Ventura could make his final appeal that a vote for Ventura was "not wasted" and would "show the establishment." The tour started on October 30 and concluded November 2. Voter turnout reached sixty-one percent and Ventura won the election with a plurality vote of thirty-seven percent.

Finances

The biggest hurdle to all campaigns is adequate finances. Although Minnesota publicly funds campaigns and limits campaign expenditures if candidates accept public funds, candidates must raise money. At the outset of the 1998 campaign Coleman and Humphrey accepted public funds. This meant that both candidates limited total expenditures to approximately two million dollars (Minnesota Campaign Finance and

TABLE 1	REASON TO VOTE FOR CANDIDATE		

Multiple Responses Allowed and Data is Percent of Responses

FACTOR	Coleman	Humphrey	Ventura
Character	27	28	44
Person	33	27	39
Party	37	53	10
Ideology	39	37	23
Record	33	59	08
Different	12	13	75
Not Typical	00	06	94
No One Reason	29	36	35
Educ. Policy	17	79	04
Abortion Position	66	27	07
Crime Policy	76	24	00
Budget Surplus	52	34	14

SOURCE: SCSU Survey. St. Cloud State University. 1998.

TABLE 2	INDIVIDUAL EXPENDITURES	
Coleman		$2,168,383
Humphrey		$2,165,294
Ventura		$626,067

SOURCE: Candidate filings with Minnesota Campaign Finance and Public Disclosure Board, 1999.

Public Disclosure Board, 1999). Coleman received $559,670 and Humphrey received $603,544 (Minnesota Campaign Finance and Public Disclosure Board, 1999). The difference between total expenditures and the public subsidy comes from a variety of sources: individuals, lobbyists, political action committees, and the state party. Table 2 shows individual candidate campaign expenditures for Coleman, Humphrey, and Ventura. Although the candidates are not required to report a breakdown of expenditures, we estimate about one-half of total expenditures were for media. If an election lacks an incumbent, it is normal for candidates spend their resources developing name recognition and answering opposition attack advertisements.

An important component of any education of a campaign is the source of candidate contributions. Table 3 shows the breakdown of sources of candidate campaign contributions. Contrary to popular wisdom, the majority of income came from individual contributions (excluding the public subsidy), not political action committee contributions. In terms of total income, Coleman received approximately two percent of his contributions from political action committees and lobbyists. Humphrey received approximately six percent of his total receipts from political action committees and lobbyists. Ventura made contributions from political action committees and lobbyists an issue in the election. He argued that these contributions, which he refused to accept, corrupted campaigns and elected officials. The data clearly shows that candidate committee revenues are nearly free of such contributions.

Coleman and Humphrey qualified for public funding because their parties successfully competed in previous elections and they each raised approximately sixty thousand dollars in fifty-dollar contributions (Minnesota Campaign Finance and Public Disclosure Board, 1999). In order to receive the public campaign subsidy, candidates

TABLE 3	CANDIDATE RECEIPTS		
	Coleman	**Humphrey**	**Ventura**
Individuals	$1,881,480	$1,415,014	$392,433
Lobbyists	$23,268	$68,324	$0
Party	$11,160	$20,000	$1,585
PACs, Political Funds	$11,499	$58,412	$1,213*
Public Subsidy	$559,670	$603,544	$308,840
Total	$2,487,077	$2,165,294	$704,071

SOURCE: Candidate filings with Minnesota Campaign Finance and Public Disclosure Board, 1999.

*Ventura did not accept PAC money. This figure is solely political fund contributions, not PACs.

must show they are viable competitors by raising approximately ten percent of the estimated public contribution. As candidates of major parties, Coleman and Humphrey each received their allocation at the beginning of the general election campaign. A candidate's public allocation follows a complex formula that takes into account past party successes and voluntary contributions that Minnesota income tax-payers make to the party of their choice when paying their annual taxes.

Coleman and Humphrey also received financial support from their respective parties. In total, the Republican party spent $5,301,392 on Coleman's campaign and the DFL party spent $3,053,903 on Humphrey's campaign. Minnesota law allows parties to support their candidate's campaigns with soft money. Party expenditures can be for direct support of candidates through general advertising or mailing absentee ballots. Candidates may form state committees that raise and spend money on behalf of the candidates. At the local level, party units (precinct and county committees) may seek financial contributions and spend those resources on behalf of the party candidates. Finally, Minnesota allows individual and organizational expenditures made independent (defined as uncoordinated expenditures) of the candidates. These expenditures are uncoordinated because there cannot be communication between the candidate and the individual or organization making the expenditure. Table 4 shows the breakdown of party expenditures for the three candidates. Table 5 is a breakdown of party funds.

Ventura's campaign coffer was not as full. From January (when Ventura announced his bid) to July (when he formally filed as a candidate) he raised twelve thousand dollars. In order to qualify for a public subsidy he needed to raise thirty-five thousand dollars in fifty-dollar increments by the end of August (Minnesota Campaign Finance and Public Disclosure Board, 1999). Ventura's subsidy was $308,840 (Minnesota Campaign Finance and Public Disclosure Board, 1999). Ventura only received about one-half the subsidy Coleman and Humphrey each received because taxpayer contributions to the Reform party were lower than contributions to the Republican and DFL parties. This obviously puts a relatively new party's candidate at a major disadvantage.

Consistent with the campaign strategy of challenging established politicians, Ventura sold black and lime-green tee shirts with the slogan, "Retaliate in '98," at the Minnesota State Fair for twenty dollars. The tee-shirt sale operation raised sixty-two thousand dollars. Thus, the campaign raised enough to qualify for its subsidy. However, the campaign would receive the subsidy *after* the election and only if Ventura received five percent of the vote. Furthermore, Ventura could not exceed

TABLE 4	PARTY EXPENSES		
	Republican	**DFL**	**Reform**
Expenditures	$4,525,621	$2,589,423	$10,068
St. Candidate. Cmtes.	$124,771	$106,689	$3,520
Party Units	$201,000	$34,714	$560
Ind. Expenditures	$451,000	$323,077	$0
Total	$5,301,392	$3,053,903	$14,148

SOURCE: Candidate filings with Minnesota Campaign Finance and Public Disclosure Board, 1999.

TABLE 5	PARTY REVENUE		
	Republican	**DFL**	**Reform**
Contributions	$5,214,123	$3,033,949	$8,126
Loans	$126,379	$0	$0
Misc.	$9,770	$80,575	$4,927
Total	$5,350,272	$3,114,524	$13,035

SOURCE: Candidate filings with Minnesota Campaign Finance and Public Disclosure Board, 1999.

the $2,200,000 expenditure total. Although the campaign finance law attempts to equalize candidate campaigns, it is clear the established parties receive preferential treatment.

In terms of Ventura's total receipts, about one-half (the other one-half came from the public subsidy) came from individual contributions. The majority came late in the campaign from a fund raising effort operated on the Internet. Ventura tried to obtain support from the national Reform party but failed to win Ross Perot's enthusiasm. Nonetheless, the Minnesota Reform party expended approximately fourteen thousand dollars on Ventura's behalf. The amount pales in comparison with the five million spent by the Republicans and three million spent by the DFL party. One of Ventura's anti-establishment claims was his unwillingness to accept contributions from lobbyists and political action committees. Table 3 shows that Ventura did not take contributions from those sources.

Reaching the fundraising threshold for the public subsidy was the first major milestone necessary to fund the campaign. The second was obtaining a loan to finance television advertisements. Coleman and Humphrey were able to pay for advertisements directly. Ventura needed to borrow funds with the anticipation he would receive his public subsidy. At first, Ventura was unable to find a bank to loan his campaign the necessary amount, about three hundred thousand dollars. Once he reached twenty percent in the polls, Steve Minn (a member of the Reform party and Minneapolis Council Member) located a bank (Franklin National) willing to make the loan. In case Ventura did not reach the vote total threshold (five percent) to receive his public subsidy, the campaign took out an insurance policy on the loan.

Although Humphrey and Coleman outspent Ventura by a ratio of three to one, he did not need to spend campaign resources to construct an image nor build name identification. Humphrey and Coleman had to spend resources to accomplish both of those goals. Ventura's campaign lacked a large paid staff, polling ability, and even a fax machine. As it turned out, it did not matter.

Internet

A relatively new campaign tool is the Internet. Ventura used the Internet for several reasons. It was an inexpensive and efficient use of valuable campaign resources. It allowed Ventura to broadcast his message without interference. If a problem arose, such as Ventura's comments about the possibility of legalizing marijuana and prostitution, his home page provided a place to make immediate clarification.

The Ventura Home Page was probably not the best constructed but it did contain many pictures of Ventura campaigning and "taking on the establishment." One of the links was to a chat room where potential voters could communicate with campaign volunteers and other potential voters. The Home Page, with links, also served as a vehicle for fundraising. Contributions of fifty thousand dollars and loans equaling forty thousand processed through the Web site.

Ventura's Geek Squad volunteers maintained the site. They videotaped campaign events and downloaded them almost immediately. The volunteers also constructed and maintained the JesseNet, an electronic mailing list of three thousand names. The list enabled quick fundraising and campaign rally organization. The most effective use of JesseNet occurred prior to the Drive to Victory Tour. The net provided the communication device the campaign used to send instructions to the drivers and other volunteers. Potential voters unable to participate in the Tour were able to watch almost on a real-time basis. The Geek Squad traveled with the Tour, taking pictures and immediately loading them on the Home Page.

The JesseNet played an invaluable role for communicating to supporters to counteract what Ventura's advisors regarded as bad or inaccurate press. For example, when Ventura noted he thought legalized prostitution and marijuana smoking should be considered, the press reported that he favored legalization of prostitution and marijuana smoking. Humphrey and Coleman immediately attacked Ventura on his outrageous statement. Within hours, however, the Geek Squad sent out the message that Ventura did not think legalization of prostitution and marijuana is good but that the idea should receive thought and reflection.

At different times during the campaign, reporters asked Ventura why he was making such extensive use of the Internet. The reasons are telling. In addition to its inexpensive cost, the vast majority of users are individuals aged eighteen to thirty. Ventura knew his campaign would be unsuccessful without those voters. Thus, Ventura took his campaign to those voters using a medium they readily understood. Minnesota is a "wired" state. Minneapolis is thought to rank among the highest "wired" cities in the United States.

Media

Ventura's media campaign began well before he officially filed as a candidate. Almost one year before the election, Ventura enjoyed free radio air time as a talk show host on KFAN, an am Twin Cities station. While hosting his show, he laid the ground work for his anti-establishment campaign. He railed against government regulations and excessive intrusion. He criticized politicians for their willingness to use tax funds to construct a new stadium for the Twins baseball team and their unwillingness to return the growing state tax surplus. After January 1998, he became more vocal in his daily attacks against "politics as usual." However, when Ventura officially filed as a candidate in July 1998, KFAN took him off the air. KFAN, similar to any radio or television station, must legally offer equal air time to all political competitors.

The campaign's resources did not allow Ventura to begin media advertising until September. It was not until the Franklin National Bank agreed to loan the campaign three hundred thousand dollars in anticipation of the public subsidy that Ventura was able to purchase extensive television coverage. In September, the campaign hired Bill

Hillsman, a Twin Cities media consultant. The campaign wanted to hire Hillsman but he was working for state Senator Johnson. When Johnson lost the DLF primary, Hillsman became available.

Bill Hillsman had a long history of developing comical and irreverent media campaigns. He worked for Senator Wellstone's 1990 campaign and is credited with creating some of the best advertisements in the country that year. Of the five DFL primary candidates, the most memorable advertisements are Johnson's.

We find it interesting that Hillsman has the remarkable tendency to find candidates that are relatively unknown, have little money, run as outsiders, and often win. This was the case with Wellstone's first senate bid. Although Johnson did not win the primary, he came in third and beat Mondale and Dayton. This suggests two conclusions. One, creative campaign advertising and strategy can lead to victory. Two, Minnesota voters are attracted to candidates outside the political establishment. The second conclusion is dependent on the first. Creative advertising is necessary to inform voters they have a choice between the well-funded, established candidate and the underfunded outsiders.

The first action Hillsman took was keeping Ventura in the Twin Cities. Hillsman argued that a two-hour, one-way drive for Ventura to meet the editorial staff of a local newspaper was a waste of his time. As we pointed out earlier, one half of the state's population resides in the Twin Cities metro area, and local newspapers and television stations reach about eight percent of all Minnesotans. Thus, Hillsman immediately brought focus to the Ventura campaign.

In terms of radio advertisements, they captured the essence of Ventura's campaign persona and answered questions some voters might have. For example, one radio short advertisement tried to accomplish three goals. First, it emphasized Ventura's differences with Coleman and Humphrey. Two, it reinforced Ventura's "tough guy" image. Third, it responded to the claim that a vote for Ventura was a wasted vote since he had little chance to win. The limerick used four short lines and was read while the theme song from the movie *Shaft* played:

When the other guys were cashing their government checks
He was in the Navy, gettin' dirty and wet
Well, they try to tell you he can't win
But we'll vote our conscience and we'll vote him in

Hillsman ran four different television advertisements. That's it! The first advertisement was "soft." A picture of the American flag appeared on screen and the voice-over told voters that Humphrey and Coleman's partisan fighting was hurting Ventura's efforts at unifying the people of Minnesota. The second advertisement was almost singularly unique. It pictured two action figures. The Ventura figure, appearing in a business suit, argued with the second figure dressed as the "Evil Special Interest Man." The Evil Special Interest Man tried to give Ventura money. The Ventura figure responded, "I don't want your dirty money," and then socked the Evil Special Interest Man. One of the themes of Ventura's campaign was that he would not accept campaign contributions from lobbyists or political action committees (PACs). He argued that lobbyists and PACs corrupted government.

The third advertisement, again, made use of the action figures. This time they were preparing a War Wagon. The advertisement prepared Minnesota for the Tour.

The fourth advertisement ran the Sunday before the election and is sure to become a classic political campaign advertisement. Once it became apparent that Ventura might actually win, Humphrey and Coleman began to point out Ventura lacked education and experience to prepare him to govern. Ventura responded that he would seek highly qualified persons to help him govern Minnesota. He also quipped to journalists, "If I'm stupid, why can't Humphrey and Coleman win?" The advertisement showed Minnesota voters that Jesse Ventura was no longer Jesse "The Body" Ventura™ but now was Jesse "The Mind" Ventura. The advertisement had Ventura sitting on a rotating pedestal, with his back to the screen. Slowly the pedestal rotated until he fully faced forward. At that point, it was clear Ventura simulated Rodin's *Thinker* statue. Once he had fully turned to the screen, he winked. On Tuesday, November 3, Ventura won the election with thirty-seven percent of the vote and, as he said , "We shocked the world!"

A final component of the media campaign was unexpected. Television, radio, and newspapers gave Ventura a "free ride." Ventura was not given the same coverage and scrutiny as Humphrey and Coleman. Broadcast and print media saw Ventura as an unlikely candidate and unable to win until September. At that point, Ventura was surging in the polls and the media reported he had a real chance of upsetting the Minnesota political establishment. This merely assisted Ventura's gubernatorial quest. However, it was too late for media to investigate and question Ventura about his policy pronouncements. It was too late to ask for clarification of Ventura's constant "don't know" answers to policy problems. It was too late for media to probe Ventura's background. They asked these questions of Humphrey and Coleman and investigated their backgrounds but not Ventura's.

Discussion Questions

1. How does Minnesota campaign financing compare with other states? Do other states provide gubernatorial candidates with public funding?

2. How do Minnesota campaign finance laws compare with similar laws at the national level?

3. What did Ventura do to capture the middle-class vote, youth vote, and female voters?

4. Considering what you read, did Ventura's advertisements correspond to his campaign statements and tactics?

5. Compare and contrast how the three candidates used media in their campaigns.

References

Lowi, Theodore J. and Benjamin Ginsberg. 1994. *Democrats Return to Power: Politics and Policy in the Clinton Era.* New York: W.W. Norton and Company.

Minnesota Campaign Finance and Public Disclosure Board. 1999. State of Minnesota.

Minnesota Poll. 1998. *Star Tribune Tracking Poll.* Minneapolis, MN.

SCSU Survey. 1998. *Annual General Purpose Statewide Survey.* St. Cloud State University.

4

Who Voted and Why They Voted

Around midnight, Tuesday, November 3, 1998, Jesse Ventura appeared in front of his supporters and uttered the famous words, "We shocked the world!" thereby declaring victory in his unlikely gubernatorial bid. Exit polling usually allows political pundits and news reporters to speculate who wins an election soon after the polls close. Although exit polling showed Ventura with a substantial lead, he did not claim victory until late into the evening. Neither Humphrey nor Coleman conceded defeat until shortly before midnight. The reason Humphrey and Coleman waited to concede defeat is simple. They incorrectly assumed either one would defeat Ventura.

Ventura's election is the biggest victory of a third party in Minnesota since Floyd Olson, a populist Farmer-Labor candidate, beat Republican and Democrat party challengers in 1930. Ventura is the first Reform party candidate to win a major public office anywhere in the country. How did he win? He is not a liberal. He does not support gun control nor government assisted child care. He is not a conservative. He supports abortion rights and the rights of gays. He is not really a centrist. A centrist would never articulate positions such as favoring abortion rights and eliminating minimum wage laws. As a candidate he never stayed on issue and always deflected tough questions about policy positions from his competitors and the media. Nonetheless, Ventura obtained 773,713 (37 percent) votes, Coleman received 717,350 (34 percent) votes, and Humphrey ended with 587,528 (29 percent) votes (Minnesota Office of the Secretary of State, 1998).

Who Voted

Key to Ventura's win was high voter turnout, especially among new voters. Turnout hit sixty-one percent (Minnesota Office of the Secretary of State, 1998). Of all voters, sixteen percent registered on election day (Minnesota Office of the Secretary of State, 1998). Of those, three out of four voted for Ventura. One of the St. Paul precincts reported that one hundred fifty of six hundred total voters registered on election day. Ventura's success was partially due to his ability to obtain the plurality in the greater Twin City area (Minnesota Office of the Secretary of State, 1998). Ventura lost only one county within a one hundred mile radius of Minneapolis-St. Paul (Minnesota Office of the Secretary of State, 1998).

Equally important to high voter turnout was Ventura's ability to attract women, youth, and the middle class. Table 6 shows that, as Ventura expected, males supported his candidacy. It is interesting that males supported Coleman equal to Ventura. Although Humphrey obtained the plurality of women voters, Ventura was competitive. At the outset of the campaign, Ventura's advisers thought their candidate's loud and brash style would offend female voters. However, Ventura's comments about abortion and gay rights attracted female voters to his campaign. The data suggests that strategy was successful.

In terms of attracting young voters, the data clearly indicates Ventura was successful. Forty-six percent of voters aged eighteen to twenty-nine voted for Ventura. The only age cohort that did not support Ventura was those voters over the age of sixty. They overwhelmingly supported Humphrey. Ventura led in the thirty to forty-four age

TABLE 6 — HOW MINNESOTANS VOTED—DEMOGRAPHICS

(Percentages)

	All	Humphrey	Coleman	Ventura
Gender				
Male	50	21	39	39
Female	50	36	29	35
Age				
18-29	16	16	37	46
30-44	32	22	32	44
45-59	29	33	33	33
60 and over	21	40	37	23
Income				
Less than 15K	7	28	29	40
15-29,999K	20	31	31	38
30-49,999K	25	26	34	39
50-74,999K	24	31	28	41
75-99,999K	12	29	34	36
Over 100K	12	20	52	28
Education				
Less than HS	7	32	36	31
HS Grad.	25	29	24	44
Some College	24	19	36	45
College Grad.	27	26	36	37
Post Graduate	18	44	38	18
Party Identification				
DFL	37	56	10	33
Republican	33	5	66	28
Independent	30	18	28	52
Ideology				
Liberal	18	45	9	44
Moderate	50	32	27	40
Conservative	32	12	58	29

SOURCE: The Star Tribune/VNS Exit Poll of probability sample of 797 voters leaving the polls around the state on election day. VNS is an association of ABC News, CNN, CBS News, Fox News, NBC News, and the Associated Press. Sampling error is approximately plus/minus 5% at a 95% level of confidence. A hyphen indicates too few respondents to analyze.

group and tied with Coleman and Humphrey in the forty-five to fifty-nine age cohort. Ventura's success in obtaining the middle class is clear. The only income group that did not support Ventura were those individuals that reported earning over one hundred thousand dollars per year. Coleman overwhelmingly captured those voters. The problem for Coleman was that voters earning incomes over one hundred thousand per year only accounted for twelve percent of all voters.

Table 6 also breaks down voters by education attainment. Ventura did not obtain the plurality of voters with less than a high school education nor those with post graduate degrees. Coleman obtained the plurality of voters with less than a high school degree and Humphrey captured the votes from those with post graduate degrees. Those with high school degrees and some college overwhelmingly supported Ventura. Those voters comprised about one-half of all voters.

As expected, over one-half of those voters identifying with the DFL party supported Humphrey and approximately two-thirds of Republican party identifiers voted for Coleman. Ventura was able to obtain the votes of one-third of DFL and Republican identifiers. Ventura captured over one-half of those voters who claimed independent status. Humphrey insisted Ventura be included in the statewide debates because he thought Ventura would take Republican votes away from Coleman. The data shows that Ventura took more voters from Humphrey than Coleman, but not greatly disproportionate. In terms of ideology, Ventura and Humphrey equally split the liberal vote. Ventura overwhelmingly captured the moderate voters and Coleman clearly was the favorite of the conservative voters. Capturing the moderate voters was key to Ventura's success, and about one-half of all voters placed themselves in the moderate category. Overall, Ventura's support was broad-based.

Why They Voted

Understanding an election outcome requires an examination of the reasons why the voters cast their ballots for a particular candidate. We showed in chapter four that potential voters preferred the positions of Humphrey and Coleman on most issues over Ventura's positions. Table 1 (see chapter four) also shows most potential voters preferred Ventura, the person, over Coleman and Humphrey. This was a key element to Ventura's election.

In addition, respondents were asked, in an open ended, multi-response format, why they would vote for their preferred candidate. Forty-four percent noted they liked Ventura's "character," while twenty-eight percent liked Humphrey's and twenty-seven percent preferred Coleman's character. Ventura campaigned on the notion that he is honest and will "shake up" entrenched political interests. We suggest this message was heard by Minnesota voters and enough of them accepted this premise and selected him to serve as governor.

Of the respondents that mentioned they liked the candidate as a "person," thirty-nine percent liked Ventura, whereas Coleman was preferred by thirty-three percent and Humphrey by twenty-seven percent (SCSU Survey, 1998). We find this rather interesting. Ventura's campaign persona was a feather-boa wearing, folding chair throwing, former professional wrestler. Coleman and Humphrey tried to convey the image of "father figures." The traditional rules of political combat suggest voters prefer a father-type person to a profane Terminator. In this election, the traditional rule of what type of person should win did not apply. Ventura faced two father-type candidates that failed to make a successful appeal to the voters to send a traditional politician to the Governor's Mansion.

Of the respondents that said they would vote for a candidate because he is different, the SCSU Survey (1998) found that seventy-five percent planned to vote for Ventura. Ninety-four percent indicated they would vote for Ventura because he is not a typical candidate. We suggest that the voters, when they compared the three candidates, clearly preferred someone different from "politics as usual." Ventura's persona is clearly different from most, if not all, politicians. Ventura offered the voters a unique choice. In this election, the voters opted for a new, different, and atypical candidate.

In terms of what voters said motivated them to cast a ballot for the candidates after they voted, it is useful to examine exit polling. Table 7 shows exit polling data broken down by candidates and issues. The voters were asked if candidate issue position aided in their vote decision. First, general farm policy and gun control had no measurable influence on voter choice in this election. Coleman's position on abortion helped him gather seventy-one percent of the twelve percent of the electorate that voted based on the issue. Coleman also did well with those voters who preferred his position on state taxes. Ventura captured a majority of votes due to his position on crime and drugs and he received a plurality of votes from those that voted due to his position on the economy and jobs. Humphrey obtained a majority of votes cast due to his position on education.

Voters also were asked how they voted based on whether they thought it should be easier to carry and conceal handguns. Only nineteen percent thought it should be easier to "conceal and carry." Of those voters, fifty-three percent voted for Ventura. Almost eighty percent of the voters indicated that it should not be easier to "conceal and carry." Those voters split their votes approximately equally among the three candidates.

The voters also were asked about the use of tax funds to build a professional sports stadium. Only fifteen percent noted that it would be acceptable to them to use tax funds for this purpose. Of those voters, forty percent voted for Coleman. The majority of the voters noted that tax funds should not be used to construct a professional sports stadium and the plurality of those voters indicated they voted for Ventura.

Ventura received the votes of the plurality of voters who saw their family financial situation better or worse than two years ago. Those who evaluated their family situation the same as it was two years ago supported Coleman. We suggest that those voters who indicated they are better off today than two years ago were willing to take a chance on Ventura. We think those voters who are worse off saw Ventura as an opportunity for positive change. Those voters who saw their financial status the same as two years ago made a safe choice and voted for Coleman, an established political commodity.

In terms of the state's current economic condition and future, a plurality of voters who saw the current economy as excellent or good voted for Ventura. Of the few (nine percent) voters who evaluated the state's economy as "not so good," a majority voted for Ventura. Again, we speculate the voters evaluated Ventura as someone who could institute change. A plurality of those who saw the State's economic future as "better" voted for Ventura. Interestingly, those who saw the future

TABLE 7	HOW MINNESOTANS VOTED—ISSUES			
	(Percentages)			
	All	**Humphrey**	**Coleman**	**Ventura**
Issues that Mattered Most				
Farm Policy	5	—	—	—
Gun Control	5	—	—	—
Abortion	12	15	71	14
Crime/Drugs	6	23	22	55
State Taxes	28	14	45	40
Education	23	56	15	27
Econ./Jobs	10	25	29	45
Make Carrying Concealed Weapon Easier				
Yes	19	7	39	53
No	79	35	32	32
Use Taxes to Fund Pro Sports Stadiums				
Yes	15	27	40	33
No	83	29	32	37
Family Financial Situation Versus Two Years Ago				
Better	42	30	31	38
Worse	13	18	31	49
Same	44	30	36	33
State's Economic Condition				
Excellent	14	33	32	35
Good	75	29	34	36
Not so Good	9	14	31	52
Poor	1	—	—	—
State's Economic Future				
Better	26	31	26	42
Worse	16	17	43	37
Same	58	30	35	35

SOURCE: The Star Tribune/VNS Exit Poll of probability sample of 797 voters leaving the polls around the state on election day. VNS is an association of ABC News, CNN, CBS News, Fox News, NBC News, and the Associated Press. Sampling error is approximately plus/minus 5%, at a 95% level of confidence. A hyphen indicates too few respondents to analyze.

economy as worse leaned toward Coleman. Of the fifty-eight percent of voters who saw the State's economy staying the same, Ventura and Coleman each received support from thirty-five percent of those voters, and Humphrey favored by thirty percent.

Table 8 shows that Coleman would have won if Ventura had not entered the race. Voters were asked, if the choice was only Humphrey and Coleman, whom would they

TABLE 8		HOW MINNESOTANS VOTED—OTHER INDICATORS		
		(Percentages)		
	All	**Humphrey**	**Coleman**	**Ventura**
If the Choice was only				
Humphrey and Coleman				
Humphrey	39	71	1	27
Coleman	47	1	69	29
Not Voted	12	0	3	94
Job Approval—				
Congress				
Approve	42	24	42	34
Disapprove	53	32	27	39
Job Approval—				
President Clinton				
Approve	58	41	18	40
Disapprove	39	9	58	32
1996 Presidential				
Vote				
Clinton	50	50	13	35
Dole	34	5	70	25
Perot	9	11	14	75
Other	2	—	—	—
Non Voters	6	8	29	62

SOURCE: The Star Tribune/VNS Exit Poll of probability sample of 797 voters leaving the polls around the state on election day. VNS is an association of ABC News, CNN, CBS News, Fox News, NBC News, and the Associated Press. Sampling error is approximately plus/minus 5%, at a 95% level of confidence. A hyphen indicates too few respondents to analyze.

have selected? Twenty-nine percent indicated they would have favored Coleman and twenty-seven percent said they would have voted for Humphrey. The data shows a "yes" answer to the question of whether Ventura brought new voters to the polls in November. Twelve percent noted that they would not have voted if Ventura was not on the ballot.

Those voters who approve of Congress' job performance tended to vote for Coleman. Those that disapprove of Congress' job performance supported Ventura. Of those voters who approve of President Clinton's job performance, forty-one percent voted for Humphrey and forty percent voted for Ventura. Coleman captured fifty-eight percent of those voters who disapprove of President Clinton's job performance. Finally, Table 8 shows that Ventura benefited by getting the support of 1996 Perot voters and new voters. Fifteen percent of the voters had either voted for Perot or not voted in 1996. Of the Perot voters, seventy-five percent voted for Ventura. Of those that did not vote in the 1996 Presidential election, sixty-two percent voted for Ventura. Those voters who supported Clinton in 1996 tended to vote for Humphrey and those that voted for Dole cast their ballots for Coleman.

What It All Means

The election of Jesse Ventura suggests a number of conclusions. Clearly, a third party candidate can win elective office in American politics. However, they must compete on a level playing field. In particular that means all candidates spend about the same amount of money on their campaigns. Coleman and Humphrey outspent Ventura. The Republican party and the DFL party outspent the Reform party. Nonetheless, spending was not as out of balance as it could have been if Coleman and Humphrey spent all they could raise. In other words, outspending the competitors does not guarantee victory. At the same time, spending less may spell defeat if a credible campaign can not be waged. Ventura spent less, but he spent enough to run a credible campaign.

Ventura's candidacy and campaign were unusual. Ventura is an entertainer and he campaigned as an entertainer. He emphasized style over substance. He played down the importance of policy debate in a campaign. He introduced mildly foul language in a bland campaign. He had fun. Ventura also had the support of a large number of grass roots activists who wanted change, and their votes elected him. Coleman and Humphrey never energized their base supporters. Yes, they had more money, activists, and professional advisers. Ventura had celebrity status and name recognition.

Ventura was able to tap into voter anger. Tolchin (1999) correctly suggests politicians have the responsibility to recognize and reconcile citizen anger. Voters are angered by many aspects of political and social life. Some people are angered by high taxes, others are offended by large bureaucracies, and still others find government regulation excessive. Throughout the nation's history, some politicians have shown the ability to recognize citizen anger and respond constructively. Often, unfortunately, citizen anger is evident but the political leaders of the day are unable to see it and properly respond.

We suggest Coleman and Humphrey failed to see that a plurality of Minnesotans are angry about various aspects of their political system and social existence. Ventura, on the other hand, recognized that some Minnesotans are angry and asked them to "show up the establishment." He successfully attacked professionally managed political campaigns and condescending elected officials. He asked voters to go to the polls and vent their anger at these mediocre politicians.

Joseph Kunkel (1999) argues that Ventura successfully tapped into an increasing American political problem. Voters are simply disgusted with politics and ordinary politicians. They believe special interests run government and the average voter lacks influence. Citizens increasingly "turn to TV including professional wrestling), video games, private pleasures and satisfactions (such as personal water craft)" instead of participating in political and community life (Kunkel, 1999). Road rage is celebrated, as is the in-your-face machismo of TV and movie characters. Today, political participation includes listening to insulting radio talk show programs and watching televised "political discussions" that are more shouting matches than rational debate. Ventura's candidacy was born on this phenomenon and his campaign strategy was structured to embrace the angry voter.

Ventura tapped into the decline in civility. He came out of the so called *new news*. He is a talk radio personality that seeks to shock. He popularized political *incorrectness* on the campaign trail. He sought to shock the voters with his outrageous statements. As he said, "We shocked the world!" when declaring victory.

The structure of politics in Minnesota provided the foundation for Ventura's successful candidacy. After all, how many states in the union have a "liberal college professor and something of a Newt Gingrich disciple" as its two U.S. Senators? Nonetheless, Ventura was not supposed to become elected. His election clearly shows the "weird, wild and unpredictable possibilities of politics when the citizens rise up and get involved" (Kunkel, 1999).

Kunkel (1999) makes clear sense when he argues that "Ventura is a significant development in civic participation in this country with both wonderful and dangerous possibilities. The involvement and empowerment that young people feel is wonderful. The development of a cult of personality, reliance on a strong man or *caudillo* are very troubling."

Discussion Questions

1. Is Ventura conservative, liberal, or a centrist? If a conservative, how do you reconcile his position on abortion? If a liberal, how do you reconcile his position on cutting taxes? If a centrist, how do you reconcile any of these positions?

2. Why did Ventura win? Earlier in the text, we noted that fifteen percent (332,540) of the voters registered to vote on election day and approximately seventy-five percent of them voted for Ventura. If same-day registration was not allowed or if Ventura did not capture the majority of these voters, would Ventura have won?

3. Considering the data presented in Table 8, is partisanship dead in Minnesota?

4. Political pundits and academic observers alike, find it easy to criticize Ventura for running a shallow, self-aggrandizing campaign. How different was his campaign from politically oriented talk shows and how other politicians, especially at the national level, behave?

References

Kunkel III, Joseph A. 1999. Correspondence to the Authors.

Minnesota Office of the Secretary of State. 1998. *Official General Election Vote Totals by County for Office of Governor, 1998*. State of Minnesota.

SCSU Survey. 1998. *Annual General Purpose Statewide Survey*. St. Cloud State University.

Tolchin, Susan J. 1999. *The Angry American: How Voter Rage Is Changing the Nation*. 2nd Edition. City: Westview Press.

5

Can Ventura Govern?

The basis of Ventura's ability to govern is the formal-legal powers of the governor's office and his extra-legal powers of persuasion. Ultimately, however, Ventura's success will depend on his interest and ability to exercise his legal and extra-legal powers. According to Thad Beyle (1995), the Minnesota Governor enjoys powers and authorities that place the office among the top ten or twelve states in formal powers (1995). Jesse Ventura, we argue, ranks at the top of sitting governors in extra-legal powers.

Formal-Legal Powers: Messages

The formal-legal powers of the Minnesota Governor are in the State Constitution and statute. The Constitution grants the governor "message power." In practice, this means the governor may submit to the legislature a proposed state budget and specific legislation.

Throughout the campaign, Ventura alternated between making specific promises and vague references about the budget. He clearly indicated his interest in returning budget surpluses to the taxpayers, cutting taxes, and limiting future budget growth. He alluded to what might not be in his budget by arguing in favor of greater personal responsibility. Soon after taking office, Ventura found the previous budget surplus already committed. Nonetheless, Ventura's 2000–01 budget calls for returning future surpluses through a sales tax rebate (Minnesota Biennial Budget, 1999). Almost immediately, the House and Senate began work on a possible tax rebate. The House passed rebate legislation based on the income tax, but the Senate sought a rebate of sales taxes. The real test of Ventura's ability to meet his tax rebate promise is whether he is able to bring the House and Senate together. His success in this endeavor will be due to his ability to persuade, not the legal powers of the office.

The proposed budget also includes a permanent reduction in income tax rates and elimination or reduction of various "user fees" such as automobile registration fees. On the campaign trail, Ventura argued income tax rates were too high at the lowest rate and penalized married persons at the highest rate. He proposed lowering the lowest rate from six percent to five and three-fourths percent and increasing the amount of allowable income before the low rate takes effect. He also proposed lowering the rate from eight and one-half percent to eight percent for married persons at high income levels. He also had great fun pointing out that Minnesotans paid a much higher automobile registration fee than in any neighboring state. His budget proposals seek to reduce the fee to a flat rate (about fifty dollars) instead of the current fee based on the value and age of the automobile. Again, whether he is successful will depend on extra-legal powers.

Although Ventura's proposed 2000–01 budget is larger than the 1998–99 budget, the increase is only approximately three percent (Minnesota Biennial Budget, 1999). Recent budgets have increased by approximately six percent (Minnesota Biennial Budget, 1999). Thus, the proposed budget meets a campaign promise if the legislature approves the budget. It is possible the legislature will increase Ventura's proposed spending plan. If so, Ventura would have the option of accepting the increases or vetoing the legislation.

Several spending programs in Ventura's 2000–01 budget are reduced. Ventura campaigned on the notion of increasing personal responsibility. He argued that government had grown too big and was providing too many services to individuals that they should obtain on their own. For example, he argued that university and "college students, if smart enough to get into college, should be smart enough to find resources to pay for college" besides state government. Guess what? The college tuition assistance programs received an inflationary increase. Instead, Ventura has proposed reducing several economic development initiatives, changing the mix of state dollars in federal-state shared programs so that state funds are less, and reducing several state-nonprofit partnership programs. Ventura argued that he had only two months to assemble a budget and if there are to be future additions or major reductions, they will come in subsequent years. In some respects, Ventura says one thing and does another. How long he will be able to continue doing that is contingent on his ability to use his extra-legal resources.

Finally, the message power allows the governor to submit legislation to the House and Senate for consideration. Usually the proposed budget provides the "spring board" for financial and programmatic legislation. It took two months (early January to the end of February) for Ventura and his staff to prepare actual bills that meet various campaign promises and subsequent pronouncements. The legislative session runs from January through May. Thus, Ventura gave the legislature only three months to consider his policy initiatives. Some legislators argued that three months is simply not enough time to properly consider Ventura's legislative proposals and began work on their own initiatives.

Formal-Legal Powers: Veto

The Minnesota Constitution provides the governor the power to outright veto legislation, to "item veto" legislation, and to use a "pocket veto" (Williamson, 1998). When the governor vetoes a bill it returns to both legislative chambers for a possible veto override. Both houses would need to muster a two-thirds vote. The item veto allows the governor to veto one or more items in an appropriation bill. The portions not vetoed become law. The legislature may restore vetoed items with a two-thirds vote in both legislative chambers. The pocket veto applies when a bill passes in the final three days of the legislative session but is not signed within fourteen days. The legislature cannot override a pocket veto. Historically, Minnesota Governors infrequently use the veto power. According to Williamson (1998), previous governors have only vetoed eleven bills per year (1998). We are unsure what Ventura will do and whether the legislature will override his vetoes. Throughout the campaign, Ventura argued that he would veto bills that are "bad for Minnesota" and sign those bills he deemed "good for Minnesota." He gave no definition of good and bad legislation. He did, however, indicate he would have the ability to freely pick and choose legislation for signature or veto without being encumbered with special interests. An important aspect of his populist appeal to the voters was his refusal to take campaign donations from special interests and lobbyists.

Formal-Legal Powers: Appointments

The governor enjoys the ability to appoint a large number of administrative agency top officials, called commissioners. In Minnesota, the commissioners manage agencies such as Public Safety, Transportation, Planning, and Natural Resources. In all, there are twenty-three administrative agencies or "cabinet" departments. The governor also appoints members to a wide variety of policy making boards. These include the Iron Range Resources and the Metropolitan Council. Two of the boards or semi-state agencies are also part of the governor's cabinet.

The legislature has limited the governor's ability to directly supervise the executive administrative apparatus to those agencies headed by a single individual. Thus, the governor's managerial reach only extends to the commissioner-headed agencies. This obviously imposes limits on the managerial effectiveness of the governor. We are unsure whether Ventura is able to effectively impose his will on the commissioner agencies.

Ventura has avoided one of the major errors of most new governors. He has not appointed a large number of individuals from his former campaign staff to these agencies. This was easy since he had a very small (two paid) campaign staff. According to Lorch (1986), former campaign staff are often poor agency administrators because either they lack necessary managerial talent or their egos compel them to constantly advise the governor on how to run the state (1986). Throughout the campaign, when asked whom he would appoint to executive agencies, Ventura said that he would look for the best available talent, regardless of party affiliation. The commissioners he has appointed have come from all quarters: the Reform party, Republican party, DFL party, and private industry. Only one appointee had problems. Ventura's first appointment to head the Department of Natural Resources resigned after it became known that he had received several citations for hunting and fishing without proper licenses.

Similar to what we find in other states, the Minnesota Governor lacks complete control over the executive branch. The Attorney General, Secretary of State, and Treasurer, for example, are independent of the governor. They are not Reform party officials and may have much different programmatic interests than Ventura. At the same time, only the Attorney General wields much power and the Treasurer becomes an appointee in 2002.

A breakdown of Ventura's administrative team shows that sixteen of the appointees are new to state government. Ventura retained nine commissioners from the previous (Carlson) administration. As stated, only two appointees affiliate with the Reform party. Of the remaining twenty-three commissioners, eight affiliate with the Republican party, six are DFL, and another six are independent. Three of his appointees have not publicly indicated their party affiliation. Of the twenty-five, only four have indicated they voted for Ventura. Seven said they voted for Coleman and two indicated they voted for Humphrey. Twelve failed to disclose which candidate they supported. The cabinet is largely male (sixteen) and white (twenty-four). A coalition of African-Americans criticized Ventura for not including more persons of color but he deflected the criticism. Ventura argued his search for cabinet members was solely on ability, not race, party affiliation, or gender.

The commissioners seem to have wide latitude. Ventura's management or leadership style suggests that agency heads have significant discretion. He has refused to micromanage departments. Department heads run their departments without interference from the governor. They seem to be free to represent their departments to the legislature and to the media. The only constraint the governor has placed on them is that they may not develop policy proposals for the legislature that are not in Ventura's budget. We think this means that few substantive policy initiatives will come from the executive agencies. Ventura has said little about substantive policy except for a one-time tax rebate, a lowering of several taxes and fees, help for Minnesota farmers, and a reduction in elementary school class size. He has argued for less government and more personal responsibility. Again, we conclude this means fewer legislative initiatives coming from Ventura and his cabinet departments.

Extra-Legal Powers: Public Opinion

The most important resource a governor has is public opinion. A governor can focus public attention on issues and seek public support to move the legislature in a particular direction. To be sure, not all governors are adept at forming, shaping, and using public opinion. To date, Ventura has shown he has the ability to form public opinion. We are unsure if he will be able to use the support he has in the electorate to obtain policy.

The expectations the public has of Ventura to do a good job are high. Ventura must work to meet the public's expectations. The legislature is keenly aware of how popular Ventura is among the voters and has pledged to cooperate with his administration. The Minnesota Poll (1999) reported in early February that Ventura has a favorable rating of seventy-two percent. It is very difficult for the legislature, if it wishes to have any lasting influence, to challenge a popular governor. A governor may appeal directly to all citizens in the state. The legislature lacks a similar constituency. Ventura campaigned as a populist, an outsider, and will always be able to go to the citizens to seek their support. At the same time, if his deeds fail to meet his words and he is perceived as an institutional politician, his support among the electorate will evaporate. He was able to garner a plurality of the vote because the electorate did not see him as a "regular" politician.

Normally, we would expect a popular governor to use the media to maintain his popularity by working with the journalists who maintain a vigil in the Capitol. Not Ventura. In some respects he has gone out of his way to antagonize reporters. Generally considered, this is not the best way to work with media. Most political advisers argue that media is a politician's friend. Media offers the quickest and cheapest outlet a politician has for his or her message. Antagonized reporters will investigate and report. It is an exceptional politician that can withstand constant investigation and unfriendly news reports and editorials. At first glance it seems odd that Ventura is not trying to develop a friendly working relationship with local media.

During the campaign, the media initially ignored Ventura as a viable candidate. His political and governmental experiences were discounted or seen as minor. The media reported his campaign as something of a side show to the real battle between Coleman and Humphrey. Major newspaper editorialists recommended Minnesotans vote for either Coleman or Humphrey. Yet, Ventura received valuable media coverage and used it in his appeal to the voters. As a populist or anti-establishment candidate, he was able to attack Coleman and Humphrey as entrenched politicians who had forgotten the common taxpayer. He was able to successfully place media in the same light as Coleman and Humphrey. Perhaps Governor Ventura has an interest in criticizing the media to maintain the populist image he has with the voters.

Extra-Legal Powers: Party Leadership

A governor is the leader of his or her party. As majority party leader, a governor has an existing coalition of supporters in the legislature to obtain passage of their legislative agenda. If the governor is not of the majority party, he works to oppose the majority. The tool the governor may use to oppose the majority is the veto. Former Republican Governor Arne Carlson faced DFL majorities in both chambers of the legislature and set veto records. His vetoes were sustained because the DFL did not have the two-thirds votes necessary to override. This often meant the DFL was forced to either accept a veto, and therefore lose the legislation, or pass legislation acceptable to Governor Carlson.

Ventura is faced with an interesting opportunity. He might be the leader of the Reform party but the Republicans hold the House of Representatives and the DFLers hold the Senate. Not a single Reform party affiliate holds a seat in either chamber. Thus, the tool normally available to a governor to obtain or stop legislation is not something Ventura possesses. However, Ventura may be able to build coalitions within the Republican party and the DFL party. Ventura has argued for several policy initiatives favorable to the Republicans, such as greater personal responsibility and permanent tax and fee cuts. Similarly, Ventura has indicated his support for policies favorable to the DFL, such as a tax rebate based on the sales tax and greater emphasis on public school education. It is equally important to note that Ventura's gubernatorial style is such that building legislative coalitions might not be of particular interest.

Extra-Legal Powers: Personal Background and Style

The personal and professional background of a governor often indicates how the individual will function as a sitting governor. Most governors come into the office with prior elected office experience. Early Minnesota Governors had served as Lieutenant Governor (Williamson, 1998). More recently, governors have served in the state legislature prior to their election (Williamson, 1998). In other words, governors have come to the office with statewide experience. Ventura, however, came to the office with a much different background. His only governmental experience was a single term as part-time mayor of Brooklyn Park, a suburb of Minneapolis. Beyond that, his background was in the private sector as a radio talk show host, actor, and professional wrestler. Unlike most previous governors, Ventura is neither a lawyer nor a college graduate. Does this mean that Ventura is unprepared to function effectively as Governor of Minnesota? We are unsure. We think it means that Ventura may have a rather steep learning curve (which he noted he had during the campaign) and as an uninitiated statewide elected official may commit a few errors and blunders.

In terms of gubernatorial style, Ventura is developing one all his own. There is no doubt that Ventura has great charisma. He has spent his entire life developing an entertaining persona. Jesse Ventura is not his given name. He chose it when he entered professional wrestling. As a wrestler, he developed a reputation as a "bad boy." He seeks confrontation and eschews compromise. He ran for mayor of Brooklyn Park to challenge the existing ruling establishment. One of his campaign slogans for governor was "Retaliate in '98." At times it appears his policy interests originate solely from personal experiences. He seems confused about the differences between private citizenship and public life. He says one thing and does another, and gets away with it! He seems to think that governing is about entertainment. So what does this tell us about Ventura's governing style?

Ventura's candidacy was attractive to the voters because of his Ventura's persona and anti-establishment views. This allows Governor Ventura to challenge the legislature and to take risks and offer innovative policy and governmental procedural ideas. As an outsider, Ventura is able to communicate to the legislature his general philosophy about government and what that means in terms of substantive legislation. Beyond that, Ventura believes the daily work of drafting legislation is the job of the legislature, not the governor. As an example, Ventura told the legislature he would like to see a tax rebate based on the sales tax. The Republican controlled House quickly passed a tax rebate based on the income tax. A legislator told Ventura that he needed to work and negotiate with the legislature, so the legislation that eventually comes to him will be something he can sign. If not, and Ventura vetoes the legislation, he would take the chance of a successful veto override. Ventura indicated that he did not care. He noted his disinterest in negotiating with the legislature and seems confident that he can go to the public and seek their support. This approach indicates Ventura is a "hands-off" governor. Ventura campaigned on the premise he would be a "hands-on" governor.

Ventura's first veto suggests his libertarian philosophy may play a role in his approach to governing. The Republican House and the DFL Senate passed legislation requiring that all automatic lawn sprinkler systems be fitted with a (thirty-five dollar) device to shut off the sprinkler if it is raining. Ventura indicated that the idea of the device is good, but it is not something the state of Minnesota should require. He argued that turning off a lawn sprinkler when it is raining is an individual responsibility.

Ventura, the Governor, seems intent on maintaining a private life. As an outsider to politics, this seems possible. Ventura's persona and his public support allow him to engage in behaviors previous governors (and probably all other Minnesota elected officials) would not fathom as permissible. Historically, Minnesotans have reacted harshly to politicians that sought to increase their personal wealth through their office. This is not the case for Ventura. Since he is a star, an entertainer, he is able to successfully increase his wealth while in office. He argued that his spouse should be paid a salary, he signed a contract to publish an autobiographic book, and he continues to market a variety of items—action figures, tee shirts—with his name. We are unsure of the consequences of this but it does show the public remains supportive of Ventura and therefore increases his potential for political power.

At the same time, Ventura's interest in maintaining separation between his private and public life is troubling. It may be too easy for his private life to overtake his public duties. One role Ventura seems to enjoy is that of entertainer. He once remarked, while mayor of Brooklyn Park, that he was not about governing but only interested in entertaining. We find this a bit troubling. An elected official works for the people. Too often it seems Ventura's motivation is personal or private. His focus on his personal wealth is an example. He also seems motivated to change public policies he finds personally unacceptable. He entered the Brooklyn Park mayoral contest because of anger over proposed zoning changes near his home. He entered the gubernatorial race because he did not receive a rebate from previous tax surpluses. He has asked for a reduction in automobile license fees because his are too high.

As an entertainer, it seems reasonable to engage in actions to draw attention. As governor, however, words and deeds that draw attention but are not accurate or truthful are problematic. Ventura constantly suggests he does not meet with lobbyists. Bashing lobbyists was a terrific play by an anti-establishment candidate on the campaign trail. It made for one of the most memorable campaign commercials of 1998. The fact is, many lobbyists were on his transition team and continue to have access to his office. He stated in his first State of the State address that governmental regulations are excessive, pointing out a rule dictating how butter must be spread on bread in a Minnesota nursing home. Statements such as these make terrific newspaper copy. The problem is that no such regulation exists.

It seems problematic for Ventura to remember that all actions he takes are now public. Private citizens have private conversations and may even appear on late night television talk shows and "joke" about the behaviors of ethnic groups in society. As governor, private conversations are far and few. The telling of ethnic "jokes" is not acceptable behavior. Nonetheless, Ventura's ability to mold and shape public opinion seems to be his greatest asset and might enable him to be a successful governor.

Discussion Questions

1. Compare and contrast Governor Ventura's "message" powers with similar powers in other states and with those of the American President.

2. Compare the veto powers enjoyed by the Minnesota Governor with other states. How does Minnesota rate? Why might one governor extensively use the veto and other governors rarely use that legislative tool?

3. What will happen to Ventura's governorship if he is unable to form and shape public opinion? How do politicians form and control public opinion?

4. Is it possible govern in much the same way as one behaved as a candidate? Is it even desirable?

5. What is the prognosis of Ventura's governorship?

References

Beyle, Thad. 1995. (Winter). "Enhancing Executive Leadership in the States." *State and Local Government Review*. Volume 27, No.1: 18–35.

Lorch, Robert S. 1986. *State and Local Politics: The Great Entanglement*. 2nd Edition. Englewood Clifts, NJ: Prentice-Hall, Inc.

Minnesota Biennial Budget. 1999. *Executive Budget Summary, 2000–01*. State of Minnesota.

Minnesota Poll. 1999. *Star Tribute Poll of How Minnesota Evaluates Ventura*. Minneapolis, MN.

Williamson, Homer E. 1998. "The Minnesota Governor: Potential for Power." In Steve Hoffman, Donald Ostrom, Homer Williamson and Kay Wolsborn, eds. *Perspectives on Minnesota Government and Politics*. 4th Edition. Edina, MN: Burgess Publishing. Pp. 29–63.